CAPTURING FULL-TREND PROFITS IN THE COMMODITY FUTURES MARKETS

CAPTURING FULL-TREND PROFITS IN THE COMMODITY FUTURES MARKETS

Maximizing Reward And Minimizing Risk With The Wellspring System

Colin Alexander

Windsor Books, Brightwaters, N.Y. 11718

Published by Windsor Books
P.O. Box 280
Brightwaters, N.Y. 11718

Manufactured in the United States of America

ISBN 0-930233-50-6

Acknowledgments

This book could not have been written in anything remotely resembling its present form without the immense contribution of Ruth Rodger. For her innumerable comments on content and style and for her encouragement I am extremely grateful.

I am also grateful to Commodity Research Bureau and Commodity Perspective for permission to reproduce their charts.

In the interests of efficient style, I have used the masculine form throughout this book.

C.A.

Table of Contents

Chapter 1

Congratulations On Your New Business!

This book shows how to establish and run a successful long-term business. Possibly the most successful long-term business that you could *ever* envisage.

The world of Futures offers more opportunity than most people are likely to find in a lifetime of looking. And it helps to know that the venture is capable of fulfilling that oft-touted claim of unlimited potential.

But Futures trading is no different from most businesses in one obvious and important respect: it has to be set up and managed in a diligent and responsible fashion. Like most businesses, its requirements are technical knowledge, capital management skills and personal discipline. Unlike most businesses, you don't have to worry about employees or customers.

So, if that's all that's required, why isn't everyone running a successful Futures trading business?

One answer is that a knowledge base that functions as a practical working tool has been very elusive. Many successful traders have been reluctant to share their secrets, or have communicated them only in bits and pieces. Many books on Futures are interesting and useful but lack instructions on how to proceed, step by step, to become a successful trader.

This book is the product of many years of experience, learning by trial and error, and searching for what seemed necessary to be explained but never was. One of its most useful features for novice traders (and for those who have not succeeded in making money from trading Futures) is likely to be the ease with which you can test the Wellspring System by paper trading. You should be able to prove the virtual certainty of making money if you follow the system's rules. Proving it on paper should help build the confidence it takes to put the signals successfully to work in the market. And successful trading is likely to lead to more successful trading.

One thing this book does not do is explain the mechanics of how the Futures industry operates. It does not duplicate what has been done so well already by those who have written the basic textbooks. With that reservation, the Wellspring System is as useful for the novice as for the experienced trader and the business person using Futures markets to offset commercial risks. Trading for personal profit and hedging both require the criteria described here for identifying markets likely to make major moves up or down, or likely to go nowhere.

FOLLOWING THE FOOTPRINTS

The Wellspring System is based on technical analysis. The idea is that the movement of prices reflects all wisdom in the market. Technicians see footprints left by other traders which suggest whether buying pressure or selling pressure is the stronger, and thus whether prices are likely to go higher or lower. Before a big move really gets under way, you can see footprints created by large traders exerting a visible influence on price as they stock up on contracts in anticipation of the move.

We can never know as much about the corn crop in Iowa or about potential demand for corn in the Soviet Union, for example, as do people directly involved in the business of trading in grains. Nor can we know the news affecting most price movements until after it has been printed or broadcast to the world. But if traders close to the business start building big Futures positions on one side of the market or the other, they cannot do so without revealing to technicians that something is happening. Traders seldom build big positions, and press the market to do so, unless they believe that a significant move in price is likely to occur. That such a movement may be self-fulfilling doesn't matter as long as they get in early.

Technical analysis can show you when to get into a market just as it's starting to move, and often long before the reason for the move becomes generally known. A student of supply and demand fundamentals may be able to tell you, in principle, what to buy or sell. But it is much more valuable to know *when* to buy and sell — and when to do nothing, which can be much of the time in most markets.

YOU DON'T NEED A FORTUNE TO START

Futures markets are open to anyone with only a small initial stake. Contrary to popular wisdom, you don't need a fortune in order to make a fortune. You can start with $5,000, although the optimum to start with is $25,000 to $30,000. With the larger amount, you can normally participate in most opportunities that arise and can achieve enough diversification to temper the risk inherent in an account trading in only one or two areas.

Apart from the somewhat greater risk carried by a very small account, the small trader is not at a disadvantage in any important sense, compared with larger traders. You can get an order filled just as fast and at just as good a price for one contract as you can for a hundred contracts.

TRADING SYSTEMS

The Wellspring System is not the only Futures trading system. But it works. Very well. Most systems claim to get you into trades with the highest probability of success, and many of them will. But most systems will also get you into an inordinate number of losing trades. An important feature of this system is that it generates relatively few signals compared with many others, except when a rapidly moving market is constantly offering opportunities to make big profits quickly.

This selectivity is very valuable: every losing trade has to be paid for with real money. So it can be almost as important not to lose money as it is to make it.

To this end, the Wellspring System will generally get you into trades likely to move with the major direction of the market. It should keep you out of most trades against the major market direction. Trading against the major trend probably loses traders more money than any other single factor. The system should also keep you out of markets likely to drift sideways. There's no point in trading a market that's not going anywhere.

It is a fundamental characteristic of trading Futures that the really big gains come from a relatively small proportion of the total trades. Therefore, it is very valuable to have a means of identifying the opportunities for very big trades early in their development. But, equally, it is vital not to lose money, on balance, in the meantime. While many other systems may not pay their way in between the big trades, Wellspring should earn you decent bread and butter profits without incurring long strings of losses or any significant drawdown in trading capital.

It is a major advantage that Wellspring operates manually, rather than by emitting signals from a computer. This lets you know what's happening. At any time you can see from charts where there are trading opportunities and whether specific trading signals are resulting in profitable trades. Too many computerized systems contain logic that is withheld from the user, making it difficult to believe in signals, particularly after a string of losses.

The Wellspring System goes back to basics. What makes markets move? What are the characteristics of their movement? And most important of all, how do we find those markets offering opportunities for profit, while avoiding those that are unfavorable?

The short answer to the last question is that we bring together many indicators that are individually valuable, and look to enter trades where there are several indicators delivering coincident signals. We also look to avoid markets where there are important indicators that negate a trade. Because it is a system with interdependent parts, you should become familiar with all of its components. If used intermittently, or if only portions of it are applied, you are likely to miss many of the best trades.

The following chapters tell you precisely, step by step, how to:

1. Identify the day to enter a trade;

2. Recognize formations for entering markets;

3. Find markets to trade;

4. Determine stop losses and liquidate trades;

5. Manage trading capital; and

6. Bring it all together.

CHECK OUT THE SYSTEM FOR YOURSELF

The best way to learn is generally by doing. The best way to bridge the gap between learning the details of the Wellspring System and putting it into practice with real money is to work through simulated trades on paper.

Some traders attach no value to simulated exercises, saying that they do not correspond to trading with real money. However, simulated trading can be compared with training airline pilots on flight simulators. There is no better way to learn without risk. Nor is there any better way to learn the rules and principles of the system, to learn to apply them and to learn to believe that they really work.

Chapter 14 shows you how to do paper trading, putting the Wellspring signals to work. For now it is enough to know that you will proceed step by step to acquire the knowledge to trade profitably. And to know that you do not have to take the system on trust and, indeed, should not. You should satisfy yourself that you personally can expect to make money by following this system.

A BUSINESSLIKE ATTITUDE

Running a successful business requires the proverbial cool head. You don't expect to be right on every trade any more than a retailer expects every piece of merchandise to sell quickly at its regular retail price. Most businesses live by a rule that 80% of the profit comes from 20% of the stock, people or invested capital.

In Futures, the 80/20 rule may mean that you have just a few enormous trades that make 80% of the profit, while a certain percentage have to be kicked out at a loss, like end-of-season merchandise. However, the most encouraging thing about Futures is, paradoxically, that 80 or 90% of traders lose money. This is paradoxical, and also remarkable, because it is not that difficult to join the ranks of the successful 10 or 20% of traders. The Wellspring System provides the knowledge. You have to supply the discipline and a small amount of trading capital to make it happen.

Having said that, the discipline should not be understated. It's obviously easy enough to accept a trade that delivers a profit equivalent to a month's or a year's pay. But some people find it difficult to take any losses. You have to learn to take them quickly, when they are small and manageable. A loss left to decrease almost always increases. Then it becomes even harder to shed. Losses allowed to get out of hand can put an end to your business. You have to accept that trading Futures is a bit like playing *Monopoly*. With planning, common sense and a little luck you can expect to get ahead. But as with the fines and rent which must be paid in *Monopoly*, Futures trading has dues which must be paid, in the form of trades that just don't work.

On the other hand, don't get carried away by the good trades! They, too, require discipline. The great stock market trader Benjamin Graham made an observation about the stock market which is even more true of Futures markets, "While enthusiasm may be necessary for great accomplishments elsewhere, on Wall Street it almost invariably leads to disaster."

You will find that trading becomes much easier once you are working with profits from previously successful trades. Until you are working with profits, you *must* be prepared to go slowly. Until you have profits, you don't know whether you personally can make Futures work for you.

TRADERS ARE PEOPLE

Appendix I at the back of the book contains an interview by Van K. Tharp with author Jack Schwager about how some traders became successful and how they continue to succeed. These factors, incidentally, aren't necessarily the same. Many people strike it rich, but it takes special knowledge and discipline to stay rich. Consistency is far more important than big wins, because the approaches that result in big wins can also result in disastrous losses.

It is particularly important to read about how other people make difficult decisions and cope with setbacks. Don't be shy about asking yourself the question, "How do other successful traders deal with this kind of situation?"

So, with the caution that you should be confident but not over-confident, welcome to the Wellspring System!

Chapter 2

Setting Up The Business

It is by no means necessary to work at trading Futures in any conventional sense of it being a full-time job. But you must regard it as a serious part-time business. This means that you should prepare yourself in a businesslike manner and undertake to do the relatively few daily tasks required to trade intelligently.

Scores of people try to trade Futures without doing the minimum homework required for making profitable decisions. These same people might spend dozens of hours buying a new car or hundreds of hours buying a house, but they won't spend half an hour a day doing the work that could build a fortune. Trading Futures without doing your homework is a loser-play.

There is no substitute for setting yourself up in a businesslike fashion at the start, just as you would for any other business. Don't cut corners. In any case, the outlay in relation to the potential for profit is minuscule.

Here's the basic list of supplies that you need:

1. *Reference Books*

   You must have a comprehensive knowledge of the way that the Futures industry operates and of its jargon. You must fully understand both the exposure to risk and the potential for gain. This book assumes basic knowledge of the industry, and it makes no attempt to duplicate the job done so well elsewhere. Even the most experienced traders would do well to have the following books for reference:

   a) *Commodity Trading Manual,* published by the Chicago Board of Trade, 141 West Jackson Boulevard, Chicago, IL 60604.
      Despite its pedestrian title, this book is easy to read and comprehensive.

   b) *Trading in Commodity Futures,* Frederick F. Horn and Victor W. Farah, published by the New York Institute of Finance, 2 Broadway, 5th Floor, New York, NY 10004.

c) *CRB Commodity Year Book,* published annually about mid-year by Commodity Research Bureau, 30 South Wacker Drive, Suite 1820, Chicago, IL 60606. This book is strongly recommended but is not essential.

2. *Weekly Charts*

You *must* have good weekly charts that go back at least ten years and that you can update each week. The best of these is probably the ten-year chart book published each spring and fall by Commodity Perspective, 30 South Wacker Drive, Suite 1820, Chicago, IL 60606-7498.

This service contains charts for 30 different Futures. Additional charts can be ordered separately.

3. *Daily Charts*

Here there are more choices. But the only useful ones are those that you can update every day for markets that you are trading or thinking of trading.

Commodity Perspective has excellent updateable charts that you can get on a weekly, bi-weekly or monthly basis. The great advantage of this service is that if you are unable to do the daily updates for a time, you can pick up the threads again when the new charts arrive.

Another choice is to make up your own charts from scratch. This is a professional approach, although it can be burdensome to catch up after not updating for a few days. Chart paper measuring 9 x 11 inches is available from Commodity Perspective. Even better, if you can find it, is a pad of paper measuring 11 x 17 inches printed with centimeter squares. The larger size allows for more weeks of price data and for larger fluctuations in price. It is useful to bind these charts with a slide-on spine.

4. *A Daily Newspaper*

You must obtain a newspaper that carries the previous day's price quotations. Outside North America the *International Herald Tribune* is widely available and carries the prices for North American markets.

5. *Weekly Price Quotations*

It is essential to have the weekly price ranges. They are printed in such publications as *Barron's* and the *New York Times*. Alternatively, you can extract this data from daily records kept for the week.

6. *Commitments of Traders (CoT)*

This information is published twice a month by the Commodity Futures Trading Commission. It is available from some quotation services and is printed in the optimum format in the Futures Chart Service published by Commodity Research Bureau, 30 South Wacker Drive, Suite 1820, Chicago, IL 60606. This feature alone justifies the cost of this publication.

7. *Miscellaneous*

a) *Pens* — Get one with a fine point that doesn't blotch. Art and drafting supply stores have the best selection. It is useful to have several colors of ink in order to draw limit moves, failed limit moves and other significant events so that they stand out.

b) *Rulers* — You need a short one for the fine work of drawing daily and weekly price bars and a 12 inch one for drawing long lines. You may also want a parallel ruler for drawing channel lines.

c) *Correction Fluid.*

Contrary to what you might imagine, it is not necessary to have your own price quotation equipment. There is considerable evidence to support the view that you are better off not to be in touch with prices during the trading day, except when your homework has indicated a possible entry or exit in a market. Fluctuations during the course of the day are more likely to be misleading than helpful if you know about them. They can turn you into a short-term trading junkie, which puts you at the mercy of floor traders. The result could be to turn an otherwise profitable trading strategy into failure. Remember that the shorter your time perspective, the less likely you are to find and hold on to the trades that make the really worthwhile profits.

Now we proceed to the heart of the matter.

Chapter 3

The Building Blocks

This chapter describes how the individual price bars that make up bar charts can be read as footprints suggesting where markets may move in the short term. Even a single bar may suggest that there is a greater weight of buying or selling in the market. Several bars taken together and put in the context of the larger picture may indicate the kind of momentum that leads to a more significant movement of price.

Bars and patterns are described here in terms of their use with daily bar charts. But the same concepts are applicable to other charts, including weekly charts, which are particularly important to the Wellspring System.

The standard reference books, such as the CBOT Manual and Horn, describe chart patterns. This chapter also does so in order to define terms used in the system, particularly because there are important small differences in the terminology in common use.

The Basic Bar is the building block for all charts. It represents the range of trading for a certain period — a day, a week or a month on printed charts, or five minutes on an intra-day chart delivered electronically from the exchanges.

The bar is set against a scale for calibration, and there is a notch on the right hand side to indicate the final price at the end of the period.

Sometimes a notch is attached to the left side of the bar to denote the opening price for the period of the bar.

The Closing Price is particularly significant for this system, depending on whether it occurs at the top, bottom or middle of the bar.

A close at either extremity suggests the direction in which the greater weight of buying or selling pressure is inclining. If the close is at the top, the greater pressure is on the buy side, and vice versa for a close at the bottom. A close in the middle is neutral, but we attribute to it the same message as the one for the previous day's close.

An Inside Day is one where trading is confined within the high and low prices of the previous day.

If traders can't push out either the high or the low of the previous day, the heavy money is presumed to be taking a rest and no significance is normally attached to these bars.

An Outside Day is one where price exceeds both the high and the low of the preceding day.

Outside days have greater significance than other days, particularly if the close is at the extremity of the day's range. It suggests that weak positions at the other end of the range have been cleaned out and that the market may continue the following day in the direction of the strong close. If the day's range has been particularly great compared with the range of recent days, the indication of direction given by a strong close assumes additional significance.

Where there is a relatively neutral close but price has substantially exceeded the previous day's high in a bull market or the previous day's low in a bear market, the market may be preparing to change direction.

*A **Closing Price Reversal*** occurs when price exceeds the previous day's high and closes below the close of the previous day, or when price exceeds the low of the previous day and closes above the close of the previous day.

A *downside* reversal is the term for this reversal when it moves from a high toward the downside (the new indicated direction).

An *upside* reversal occurs when price moves from a low toward the upside (the new indicated direction).

The closing price reversal is an important component of Wellspring's approach to entering trades. It suggests the possibility that the market may be setting up for a worthwhile move. However, there are many more reversals than there are important changes in direction, so this indicator must not be used indiscriminately.

*A **Key Reversal*** is essentially the same as a closing price reversal except that it is also an outside day, with price exceeding both the high and the low of the preceding day and closing beyond the preceding high or low.

or

(There is some variation in the definition of reversals. Some authorities describe our closing price reversal as a key reversal, particularly when price has reached far but failed to stay there.)

*A **High/Low Reversal*** occurs when price closes at one extremity of the trading range one day and at the opposite extremity the next day.

or

Although sometimes omitted from textbooks, the high/low reversal is particularly significant when followed by another high/low reversal or when one occurs soon before or after a closing price reversal.

An Accumulation Pattern comprises a pattern of bars, each having successively higher lows and, ideally, also higher highs.

During accumulation, persistent buying pressure finds buyers unable to buy as low as they could on previous days, resulting in successively higher lows and the likelihood that prices can move still higher.

An accumulation pattern can be significant regardless of where price closes each day. It is as valid on weekly bar charts as on daily charts.

A Distribution Pattern is the reverse of an accumulation pattern.

Sellers are able to sell only at successively lower prices as buyers become steadily less aggressive about how much they are prepared to pay or as buying dries up.

A Consolidation Area or Congestion Area occurs when price moves sideways. A wider band of equilibrium is also called a *trading range*. We prefer to talk about consolidation when price re-groups after a surge, particularly when it occurs as part of a sustained move. Congestion is a looser term applicable to all sideways action.

A Gap is a blank space on a chart with no direct connection to the preceding bar, or group of bars, because no trading has occurred at the intervening prices.

There are four kinds of gaps, as shown on the chart for December 1985 Coffee.

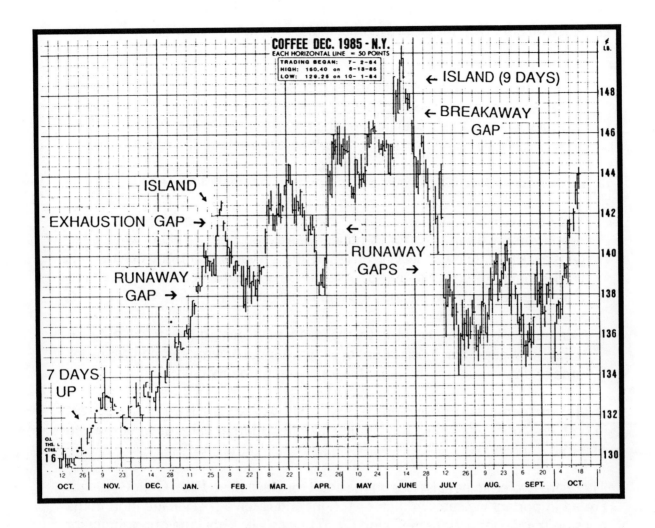

COFFEE DEC. 1985 - N.Y.
EACH HORIZONTAL LINE = 50 POINTS

TRADING BEGAN: 7- 2-84
HIGH: 160.40 on 6-13-85
LOW: 129.25 on 10- 1-84

← ISLAND (9 DAYS)

← BREAKAWAY
   GAP

ISLAND

EXHAUSTION GAP →

RUNAWAY
GAPS →

RUNAWAY
GAP →

7 DAYS
UP

a) ***A Common Gap*** can occur at any time. It has little significance, except that we consider it for emerging trading formations (described in Chapter 4).

Often occurring within a congestion area, a common gap is generally filled within a few days by price moving back to establish a connection with the other bars on the chart. But you can never be certain until after the event whether this will happen or whether you are looking at the start of a breakout.

b) ***A Breakaway Gap*** occurs when price breaks out from a congestion area and never looks back.

A breakaway gap is a reliable indicator of important buying or selling power. It suggests that a major move may be just starting. Although it can be frightening to see how far price has moved on the first day of a breakout, the rule of thumb is: the more powerful the breakout, the further price is likely to go. Consequently, there is unlikely to be another chance to enter at a more favorable price and with a more manageable risk.

c) **A Runaway Gap** occurs in a market that is continuing to tear away in a major run.

These gaps occur when a market starts to go straight up or collapses downward. They are sometimes called mid-point gaps or measuring gaps, the idea being that they will tend to show up around the mid-point of a non-stop move. This, however, is only an imprecise way to estimate the extent of a runaway move.

d) **An Exhaustion Gap** occurs at the end of a substantial move.

You can never be certain until after the event whether you have a runaway gap or an exhaustion gap. It can be identified as an exhaustion gap either when price gaps back the other way, leaving an island (the next definition), or when the gap is filled on a closing basis; that is, price closes below the bottom of the gap in a bull market or above the top of a gap in a bear market.

Sometimes you may be able to make an intelligent guess to identify an exhaustion gap when it occurs under circumstances where other indicators for time and price suggest the potential for a turn in the market.

An Island consists of one or more days of trading where there is a gap on the chart in both directions. It is often the ultimate manifestation of exhaustion at the end of a major move.

There are two prominent islands on the chart for December 1985 Coffee. Islands are an important indicator in their own right and receive special attention in the rules on trading formations in Chapter 4. They usually signal the opportunity for a profitable trade and sometimes signal the opportunity to enter a trade right at a major turning point.

Five Consecutive Closes in the same direction constitute a pattern of unusually persistent buying or selling, and suggest that it is likely to continue.

This pattern also constitutes an important indicator in its own right. You can enter right away when there is an entry signal to do so (see Chapter 4). This indicator has a reliability approaching 80% as an indicator of the major trend. When it is wrong, it may be as a result of exhaustion at the end of a major move or a major correction.

ALWAYS TRACK THE FOOTPRINTS

It is always useful to look closely at how strong or weak a market is by examining its price action. Close inspection of individual bars and groups of bars often gives vital clues that confirm a direction or that warn of a possible change in direction.

A strongly rising market tends to have the majority of closes at the upper end of the daily range. It also tends to have more days when price goes up than down. And individual advances are generally larger than individual declines.

A rising but laboring market may show aberrational behavior, despite its ability to make gains in closing prices. For example, one downside reversal day is likely to be a random aberration, especially if it is not very large. But more downside reversals than upside reversals over a period of several days or weeks suggests that sellers are asserting themselves: gains early in the day are being consistently knocked down by sellers late in the day. Consequently, there is a high probability of at least a short-term correction, if not a more significant change of direction.

Gaps constitute one of the most pronounced indicators of pent-up buying or selling pressure. One small gap within a consolidation area may mean nothing. They occur frequently and are usually filled in a day or two; hence their designation as common gaps. But the existence of several gaps up indicates the release of pent-up buying power, suggesting a market to be long. By extension, it suggests a market in which you may not want to hold short positions, even though the overall direction may be downward, unless the gaps up are filled on a closing basis (discussed in Chapter 11).

When there are several gaps down in a rising market, the uptrend is extremely suspect and you would expect to see strong signals to liquidate long positions. Often a single gap down may result in a signal to liquidate positions, particularly when price closes in the bottom 25% of the day's range.

The most treacherous of all situations can occur when there are recent gaps in both directions. These gaps suggest the possibility of a violent move, and not necessarily in the direction of the most recent gap, unless the direction is strongly confirmed by other indicators. Particularly at a potential top after a sustained move, there may be violent gapping in both directions. Under these circumstances, interpretation of individual gaps is difficult unless there is a clear gap out of a consolidation area.

While day-by-day trading action is discussed here in terms of a rising market, the concept is equally applicable when applied to declining markets and to determining the likely direction of a break out of a consolidation area.

This chapter describes the ways in which traders' buying and selling leaves footprints, as shown by individual price bars and small groups of bars. The beginning of what may turn out to be a worthwhile journey is virtually certain to be revealed by these footprints. You should, therefore, be able to recognize these patterns automatically.

In Chapter 4 we identify trading formations, which are built using the individual bars and bar groups described in this chapter. In Chapter 5 we introduce the procedures for entering trades. After that, we show how to identify markets offering the best potential for profitable trades.

As with learning another language, there are various ways of proceeding. We are moving in this sequence so that the overall concept of entering markets stands together, although it precedes the critical chapters that show how to select markets to trade.

Chapter 4

Trading Formations

One day's trading action, on its own, is unlikely to be of much use as an indicator for profitable trades. But the action of several days taken together can start to make chart patterns that show buying pressure or selling pressure.

When random buying or selling takes place in the ordinary course of business, price will tend to make random movements that lack any discernible pattern. When there is a persistent weighting of pressure toward either buying or selling, the presumption is that traders are pressing the market to build up positions or to reduce positions. We may have no idea why this happening, at least not until later, but we can readily see a pattern of strong closes in the same direction, frequently coupled with a pattern of successively higher highs and higher lows in daily ranges, or vice versa.

In short, one footprint in the sand rarely suggests a direction. When a pattern of footprints starts to point in a certain direction, the prima facie evidence suggests that the trail will continue. From this principle, we proceed to discuss trading formations — patterns comprising price bars from several days of trading, which suggest that there may be enough weight of money at work to start a bandwagon. These trading formations are described below as a set of rules.

Rule 1. The Three-Day Rule

A buy signal is delivered on completion of three consecutive days of price closing in the upper half of the day's trading range.

A sell signal is delivered on completion of three consecutive days of price closing in the lower half of the day's range.

Buy Signal   Sell Signal

The three-day rule conveys the basic concept of identifying emerging momentum. All eight trading formations discussed in this chapter are based on this concept.

All the trading formations are also subject to the following four points:

1. A trading formation is completed only when the final bar has a close in the respective top or bottom 25% of the day's range.

2. Because of the general requirement that price should close in the top or bottom 25% of the day's range on the entry day, formations may take longer to be completed than the minimum time specified by the rules. Thus, you might not have a valid entry in accordance with Rule 1 until the fourth or even the fifth day.

3. When price closes in the middle of the day's range, the result is regarded as neutral and is given the same designation as the previous day.

4. When an emerging pattern is violated, you must start counting again at the beginning of the potential trading formation.

Rule 2. The Regular Reversal Rule

Shorten the proving time for the trading formation from three days to two when either of the two trading days is a reversal of any kind — closing price reversal, key reversal or high/low reversal.

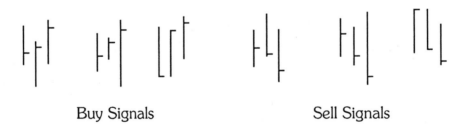

Buy Signals   Sell Signals

Rule 3. The Gap Rule

Shorten the proving time from three days to two when a gap occurs.

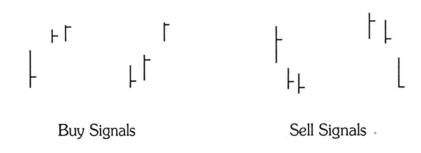

Buy Signals   Sell Signals .

Rule 4. The Island Rule

Shorten the proving time to one day when an island occurs.

Buy Signal   Sell Signal

It is not necessary for closing price(s) *within the island* to be in the top or bottom of the day's range; it is merely sufficient for the existence of the island to be clear and unmistakable. The island may consist of one day or several days, or even weeks, of trading.

Islands are a particularly reliable indicator of the end of an established trend in one direction and the beginning of a move in the opposite direction. They often indicate absolute exhaustion of the previous trend.

Rule 5. The Lindahl Rule

Lindahl Buy

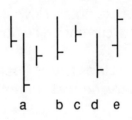

a   b c d e

Buy Signal

Within *nine* calendar days from the day of the low for the formation:

1. price must exceed the high of the bottom day for the formation: (b) must take out the high of (a);

2. price must then take out the low of the preceding day: (d) must take out the low of (c); and

3. on the entry day (e), price must take out the high of the preceding day and close above the previous day's close plus the current day's opening price.

This formation may be completed in as few as three calendar days or as many as nine, depending on how many days intervene that do not contribute to development of the formation.

Lindahl Sell

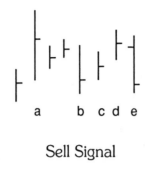

Sell Signal

Within *eight* calendar days from the day of the high for the formation:

1. price must exceed the low of the top day for the formation: (b) must take out the low of (a);

2. price must then take out the high of the preceding day: (d) must take out the high of (c); and

3. on the entry day (e), price must take out the low of the preceding day and close below the previous day's close plus the current day's opening price.

This formation may be completed in as few as three calendar days or as many as eight, depending on how many days intervene that do not contribute to development of the formation.

When a holiday occurs and the exchanges are closed during the development of a Lindahl formation, an additional day may be allowed for a valid signal to develop.

Studies by Walter Bressert show that Lindahl formations can deliver profitable signals as much as 90% of the time in Pork Bellies and Soybeans when trades are entered at expected cycle highs and lows (see Chapter 17, Cycles). While identification of cyclical highs and lows presents its own set of problems, this formation is particularly reliable for low risk entry to a trade.

Rule 6. The Trend Continuation Rule

Shorten the proving time to one day when there is a single reversal day in the direction of an *established and unmistakable trend*.

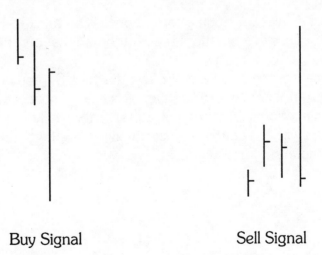

Buy Signals   Sell Signals

Traders often look at a runaway bull market or a collapsing bear market and exclaim, "Oh, I can't get into that market. I've missed it. There's too much risk now."

Wrong! It's true that it is psychologically difficult to chase a rapidly moving market. But this rule provides precisely the mechanism for getting into a fast-moving market with a manageable stop loss and with a very high probability of making a good profit quickly. (Stops are discussed in Chapter 13. The stop is just beyond the extremity of the price range on the entry day.)

This rule is also used to enter a trade on the assumption that a consolidation area within a clearly established trend is ending. When in doubt, wait another day for confirmation.

Rule 7. The Trend Reversal Rule

Trade with the new direction of a single *exceptionally powerful* reversal day against the established trend when price has reached a major target level (explained in later chapters). Exceptional power may be defined as a daily range of a limit move or more. Ideally, the opening price will have gapped away from the previous day's close before reversing.

Buy Signal   Sell Signal

Of all trading formations, this is the *least* reliable and should seldom be used because of the difficulty of defining exceptional power. Even the most powerful reversals may result in resumption of the established trend with renewed vigor.

This warning is emphasized because of the widespread view that major tops and bottoms are formed with reversal days. While this is often true, there are far more reversal days, even very big ones, than there are tops and bottoms.

23

Rule 8. The Double Reversal Rule

Enter a trade on completion of a second reversal day in the same direction within a period of about a week — whether closing price reversals, high/low reversals or a combination.

Buy Signals   Sell Signals

This rule may be used either for entry with the established trend or when other indicators suggest that a market may be at a major turning point.

As suggested by the name double reversal, this rule is essentially a repetition of previous signals: a double trend continuation rule signal (Rule 6) or a double trend reversal rule signal (Rule 7). Since double reversals occur often, are particularly reliable and can come in hybrid configurations (as illustrated), it is appropriate to recognize their importance with a separate rule.

Double reversals are often contained within Lindahl formations. The signal is much stronger if the second low is higher when buying, or if the second high is lower when selling — unless the second reversal is exceptionally powerful.

These are the eight rules for trading formations. You must learn to recognize them immediately; your response to them should be as automatic as your responses when driving a car.

The trading formations are illustrated on the chart for September 1989 Light Crude Oil. Real trades would not necessarily be taken at these points because real trades would be considered in conjunction with other indicators. Specifically, trading formations must be used in conjunction with the entry rules described in Chapter 5 and the other indicators described in later chapters.

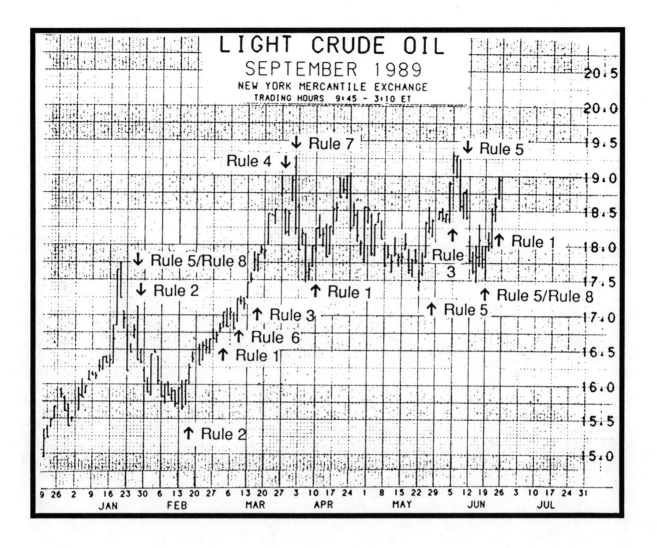

LIGHT CRUDE OIL
SEPTEMBER 1989
NEW YORK MERCANTILE EXCHANGE
TRADING HOURS 9:45 – 3:10 ET

How To Enter A Trade

Amazing as it may seem, the majority of books about Futures have little or nothing to say about the precise procedure for entering trades. One particularly scholarly 400-page book, for example, specifically avoids the issue; it says that traders must experiment for themselves with the mechanics of entering markets!

Yet no single factor is more important than knowing how to enter trades. You have to know, right at the moment of placing the order, whether you are making a responsible trade in accordance with your trading plan or whether you're taking a flyer. Trading without entry rules is like driving away from the curb without first looking to see whether the road is clear to do so.

Entry rules are described at this point in order to tie them in with trading formations. Neither trading formations nor entry rules should be applied to trading, however, without being related to the criteria for identifying markets to trade, as described in later chapters.

We have only three entry rules and they are relatively straightforward. Rule 1 is subdivided into two parts for buying and selling, although the overall concept is the same.

Rule 1(a). Buy

Buy in the last 15 minutes of the day's trading, provided that all of the following requirements are met:

a) price is expected to close in the upper 25% of the day's trading range;

b) price is expected to close above the close of the previous day;

c) price is expected to close above the opening price on the entry day; and

d) the daily price bar (the bar that will be drawn on the daily chart as a result of trading on the entry day) will complete a valid trading formation, in accordance with Chapter 4.

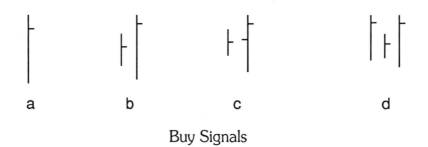

a   b   c   d

Buy Signals

Ideally, the high of the preceding day should be exceeded on the entry day, since this gives much added strength to the signal. Failure to do so does not invalidate the rule, however. There is less significance in taking out the previous day's high when entry is being considered in accordance with trading formation Rules 6, 7 and 8, as described in Chapter 4.

Rule 1(b). Sell

Sell in the last 15 minutes of the day's trading, providing that all of the following requirements are met:

a) price is expected to close in the lower 25% of the day's trading range;

b) price is expected to close below the close of the previous day;

c) price is expected to close below the opening price on the entry day; and

d) the daily price bar for the entry day will complete a valid trading formation, in accordance with Chapter 4.

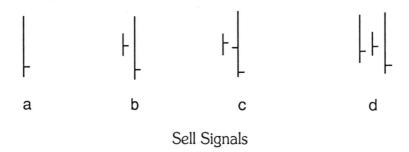

a   b   c   d

Sell Signals

Ideally, the low of the preceding day should be exceeded on the entry day, since this gives much added strength to the signal. Failure to do so does not invalidate the rule, however. There is less significance in taking out the previous day's low when entry is being considered in accordance with trading formation Rules 6, 7 and 8.

The reason for waiting to enter a trade until the last 15 minutes of the day's trading is that you want to be sure that there is real momentum in the market. We seek to enter trades that will start to deliver a profit right away. Even if they don't, at least we want to know that there is enough pressure to deliver a strong close on the entry day, since such a close increases the probability that the weight of money will return to the market in a day or two. While it may seem that you lose the opportunity for an entry at a good price by waiting to enter until near the close, you should more than make up for this apparent loss of profit by increasing the probability of the signal working, and of the trade going to a profit immediately.

Despite this strong suggestion that entries be delayed until near the close, there may be circumstances, particularly in fast moving markets, where Rule 3, the early entry rule, has advantages over this rule.

Rule 2. Limit Moves

Buy or sell, as applicable, as soon as price goes within 10% of a limit move, regardless of the time of day, provided that the resulting price bar on the daily chart completes a trading formation that delivers a signal to trade. (A limit move is the maximum allowable advance or decline from the previous day's close that is permitted in one trading session.)

Sometimes limit moves occur, particularly in Pork Bellies, which seem to come out of nowhere and which do *not* fulfill the other requirements for a trade. They should be disregarded.

On the other hand, limit moves may occur on the day when a trading formation is approaching completion. You may have identified a potential trade, only to see the means of entering whisked away from you because of a limit move. Since price will sometimes go to the limit so fast that it is impossible to enter a position before trading ceases, your recourse may be to enter the market with a buy stop or sell stop order. Your chances of entering the trade are much improved by entering a stop order 10% from the limit price. In Pork Bellies, for instance, this would be 180 points from the previous day's close, 200 points being the amount of a limit move.

The ideal is to enter a trade just inside limit and then see it lock there. But sometimes price may go to the limit, particularly early in the day, and then not hold there. Although it will probably go back to limit on the close, it is mandatory to have a stop in the market during the day in case the limit move is an expression of exhaustion, preparatory to a change in direction, or at least a consolidation. The suggested allowable retracement for a trade entered near limit is about half a limit move as a stop-loss. (Stops are discussed in Chapter 13.) Occasionally a market goes to limit in one direction and then goes to limit in the other direction — a very uncomfortable experience if you've just entered a trade at the wrong extremity.

If price goes to limit, or almost to it, but fails to close there, you should be very cautious. The move to limit may have resulted simply from floor traders running the stops, or from one or two big orders coming into the market without any follow-up to produce a continuation of the move.

The important thing about entering on a limit move is that entry should be justified by trading formations: you should be entering at the beginning of a worthwhile move, not at the end of it. On the other hand, you should not resent giving up the difference between the previous close and an entry price a limit move away. The market shows with a limit move that there is real power in it, the very thing we most want for our trades.

Rule 3. Early Entry

It is permissible to enter a trade on the opening, or during the day, when that one day alone remains to complete a trading formation, *provided that other indicators strongly support the trade.*

It can be important to use this entry rule when price gaps through support or resistance (discussed further in Chapter 11). Otherwise the market may travel a long way during the day, leaving you behind. Early entry can also work well with formations that take several days to develop, such as Lindahl formations.

Trades entered during the day must have an ordinary stop-loss entered — not a close only stop. Our approach is to place the stop after the market has been open for an hour, either just under the low to that time when buying, or just above the high when selling. Alternatively, use the respective high or low of the previous day's range as the marker for the stop. (See Chapter 13, Stop Rule 7.)

Never let yourself slip into a short-term mindset. The purpose of making an early entry is to get in at a good price for a longer-term trade when everything else is set up for it to come through. Remember that successful short-term traders don't tolerate markets going against them: most live by the rule, "Never take a loss home overnight!" You, too, should be prepared to get out if the expected signal does not come through on the close, *particularly if the trade shows a loss.*

ENTRY TO MARKETS — ADDITIONAL POINTS

There are some other points that you should know about entering trades, although they have not been codified into rules.

1. It is important to enter a trade immediately on delivery of an entry signal. Many of the best trades get under way at once and do not offer another chance to get in at a more favorable price.

2. The more powerful the signal, the more important it is to get in right away.

3. If you miss an entry signal, the best alternative is to place a market order before the opening of the next day. You can often get in around the close of the previous day's trading. In a bull market the price may open at, or slightly below, the previous day's close before starting to work higher. In a bear market the opening price may be at, or slightly above, the previous day's close.

Sometimes on the open, though, price gaps away from the previous close. While there is a very high probability of the market continuing, there is inevitably an increase in the amount of money put at risk, since the stop still has to be in the same place.

The worst thing you can do is to try and day-trade the market by second-guessing fluctuations during the day. Whatever you do is likely to give you a less favorable price, not a better one. Day-trading in any form is absolutely not recommended, except for those who have a *proven* system for making consistent profits. By and large, the only people who make money from day-trading are people on the floor of the exchange. Don't be tempted to try it!

4. A caution: the entry rules are not expected to deliver profitable trades unless they are brought together with the trading formations described in Chapter 4, as well as with the other indicators for identifying markets to trade which are discussed in subsequent chapters.

Chapter 6

Starting The Search For Markets To Trade — The Fundamentals

WHEN ARE PRICES HIGH OR LOW?

We are concerned with the technical aspects of trading Futures. But technical and fundamental considerations merge in one respect: in determining what constitutes a high price or a low one.

Fundamentalists might look for the answer to when prices are low in news reports of bankruptcies among producers. When prices are high, they might read about acute scarcity of supply, ruinous costs for consumers and abundant profits for those producers with product available to sell. Technicians such as ourselves, instead of getting ideas about trading from newspapers, look at long-term charts to see what has happened before. Ideally, we find charts going back several decades like the ones in the CRB Commodity Year Book. Otherwise, as a less desirable alternative, we use the ten-year, updatable weekly charts.

You can see from long-term price charts that most markets go through erratic fluctuations between very high prices and very low prices. This leads conservative, long-term investors to look for trades having the potential to swing from one extremity to the other over a period of at least one year, and usually several years. In short, to buy low and sell high. Or vice versa.

The economic reason for these swings is quite simple. Very low prices for a commodity will lead to bankruptcies among producers and will deter investment in new productive capacity. Therefore, supply shrinks. In due course, demand overtakes supply. So prices rise. As prices rise, consumers buy more than they might otherwise, in order to protect themselves from further price increases or supply shortages. At the same time, producers will be in no hurry to deliver to markets more than they have to: there's no point in rushing to sell something today that's likely to be worth more next week or next month.

From a producer's perspective, rising prices can lead to a situation where a lower volume of sales can produce more profit, not less. Alternatively, in the mining industry, for instance, high prices prolong the life of the mine without necessarily adding more metal to the market.

Only on reaching historically high prices will producers make every effort to deliver all that they can, while consumers do their utmost to curtail purchases. But until that level is reached, exaggerated demand squeezes diminished supplies so that prices rise far more than expected. Quite a small imbalance in the relationship between supply and demand can have a disproportionate impact on price levels.

When prices reach very high levels, new investment is attracted to the industry and, eventually, new supply comes on stream. But all of this takes time. So high prices seldom lead quickly to new supply, reduced demand and a return to very low prices.

In a declining market, producers try to sell as rapidly as possible for fear of still lower prices. Consumers reinforce the downtrend by refraining from building excess inventories that may depreciate in value. Some producers may initially decide to hang tough on declining prices. But eventually they merely reinforce the decline as they successively throw in the towel. Only upon reaching historically low prices will producers be likely to regain the upper hand by holding back enough supply to stop the decline. At these levels consumers will also step up and add to inventories at bargain prices, thus helping producers arrest the decline.

What constituted low and high prices in the past is known generally. People in the industry know because they remember well the times of feast and famine. We know from looking at charts. Thus, both fundamental traders and technicians work together so that their trading makes historically high or historically low levels a target for bull and bear markets, and a turning point.

The exception to the pattern of fluctuation of markets between a range of high and low prices occurs when the range is unexpectedly broken. If there is a breakout to the upside, there may be a burst of panic buying that takes prices far higher than ever seemed possible. In all likelihood, most producers will have sold all their available inventory before price broke out to new historic highs. Therefore, an already short supply leads to panic conditions.

When there is a similar break to the downside, below an established long-term low, there may be corresponding panic liquidation — by both producers and consumers.

You should be warned that there is a strong tendency for people to assume that prices at one extremity or the other represent a "new era." In the bankruptcy zone, people come to believe that there will never again be high demand or high prices. Gloom feeds on itself, thus reinforcing the urge to close unprofitable capacity. Similarly, in the fat-cat zone, there is no shortage of people who imagine that high prices will remain forever and who want to invest in new capacity. The "new era" psychology is usually most pronounced after a major breakout to new historic highs or after a major collapse below long-term low price levels.

Any time that you hear talk of a "new era" or "it's different this time" relating to very high or very low prices, you can be sure that the end must be approaching, with prices heading in due course to the opposite extremity.

In between the fat-cat zone and the bankruptcy zone, prices often settle in a zone of equilibrium, in which supply and demand are in approximate balance. Such situations can last for a long time, creating a so-called trading range. In these market conditions, there is no need for aggressive buying by consumers or aggressive selling by producers. No one needs to keep large inventories at any point along the pipeline between production of the raw material and delivery of the finished product. Nor does there appear to be a need for major changes in investment, either to expand capacity or to close it down. So eventually both producers and consumers become complacent.

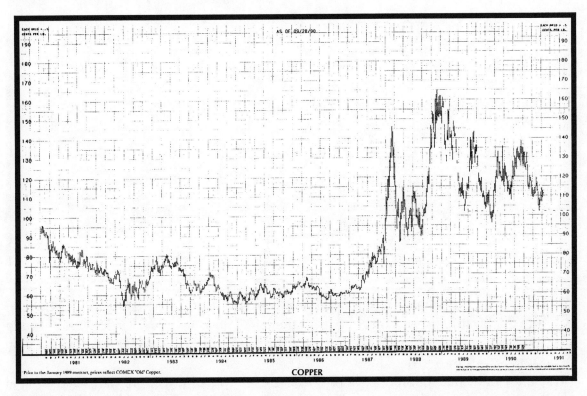

COPPER

The weekly chart for Copper shows that it was in an extended trading range for four years, from 1983 to 1987. Prices remained relatively low and stable because demand appeared to be shrinking faster than mines were closing. Fiber optics and satellites were believed to be replacing copper wire used in telecommunications; plastic was thought to be replacing copper used in plumbing; and the automobile industry was thought to be entering a "new era" of lower demand for copper.

But in due course, demand came to exceed supply, with the usual, predictable result. Since the price had been stable for a considerable time, there was little elasticity in mining capacity to accommodate a relatively small increase in demand, many unprofitable mines having been closed in the meantime. In mid-1987, the price of copper started moving sharply higher, proving the adage that the longer consumers have been lulled into complacency by stable prices, the greater the panic when that equilibrium is disturbed. Volatile markets are used to accommodating shocks, while tranquil markets are not.

Accordingly, the price of copper, once started higher, continued to rise until it surpassed its previous record high in 1980. A subsequent retracement of about half the total advance then set the stage for another successful assault on the high, setting a new record above $1.60 per pound.

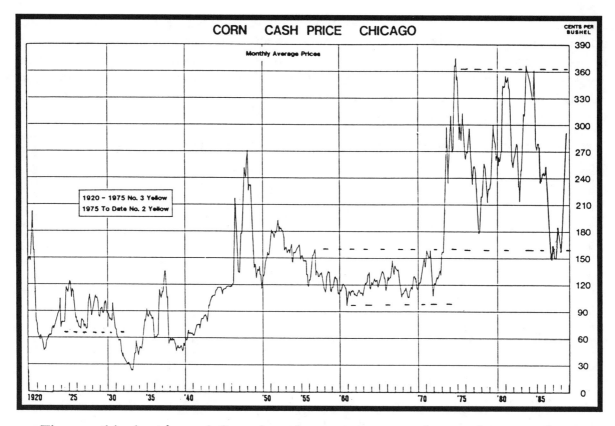

CORN   CASH PRICE   CHICAGO

CENTS PER BUSHEL

Monthly Average Prices

1920 – 1975 No. 3 Yellow
1975 To Date No. 2 Yellow

The monthly chart for cash Corn shows how price remained in a trading range between $1.00 and $1.50 for almost 15 years, from the late 1950s to 1973. Price finally broke out in 1973 and exploded to $3.75 when a complacent market was hit unexpectedly by high demand from the Soviet Union.

This enormous bull market provides a classic example of the supremacy of technical analysis over the fundamentalists trading off perceptions of supply and demand. In this case, the major new component of demand, Soviet buyers, succeeded in filling most of their requirements, by buying Futures and arranging for forward delivery of all grains, long before news of their needs came out. In these circumstances, the smart money *sells* on the news, having previously bought when the technical indicators were proving the existence of demand, from whatever as-yet-unknown source.

Major buyers or sellers frequently take positions in Futures markets large enough to affect the overall direction of prices before the news about a change in supply and demand fundamentals becomes public. It is obvious that if you want something offered at auction (which is essentially what Futures markets are), then you don't broadcast your desire to the world beforehand. The experience of what came to be known in the United States as "the great grain robbery" of 1973 and 1974 should drive home a vitally important point: it is price that signals the direction of markets when there seems to be a conflict with the fundamentals. Believe the technical indicators!

After a new high in corn prices of $3.75 was established in early 1974, everyone knew that was an established price where demand declined enough and supply increased enough to make a top. Therefore, subsequent surges in price toward $3.75 repeated the process

36

of topping near that level. Thus a new price range for corn between $3.75 and $1.50 established the zones of feast and famine.

You can also see how a range was established over a seven-year period from 1924 to 1931, when corn traded between 70¢ and $1.20. Once price fell below the lows that held during this period, it then collapsed to real bankruptcy levels around 25¢.

If you waited to see historically high or low prices before considering a trade, you might have to wait for years. Nevertheless, it is important to know where current prices are in relation to historically high and low prices. The ideal is to buy low and sell high. Far greater risk and much less potential for a long-term, high-profit trade results when buying high and selling low.

You will hear the saying (which is true) that there is no price so high that it cannot go higher, or so low that it cannot go lower. However, conservative traders should generally avoid trades where price is pushing at the limits. Markets almost always attract too many participants carried away by their emotions at the extremities; the risk of a sudden and severe correction is greater than is normally recommended for people trading Futures as a business.

In sum, avoid buying very high and selling very low. Also, look at long-term charts in order to avoid taking trades where price is confined in a relatively narrow range: major potential for profit occurs only when that equilibrium is disturbed, not before.

THE MARKET'S REACTION TO FUNDAMENTAL NEWS

There is one way that we use fundamental news as a technical indicator: we look to see how markets respond to news.

Markets should go up on bullish news and down on bearish news. If there is an established trend, the probability is that news (excluding major unexpected events) will simply push price further in the same direction. It is usual, for instance, for central banks to keep changing interest rates in the same direction once a trend is established. Similarly, a big harvest will almost always get bigger, while a small harvest will almost always shrink when successive crop estimates are announced.

If a market fails to respond to important news, it may already be in the market. Indeed, many runaway bull markets and collapsing bear markets make their final top or bottom on the very day when maximum bullish or bearish news is announced. Sophisticated traders will have had the news before its release, or will have guessed it correctly, and will have already traded accordingly. Hence the validity of the saying, "Buy on rumor; sell on news."

Alternatively, if a market fails to respond to important news, it may be that the news itself is incorrect or does not reflect true underlying supply and demand. A market that fails to respond in the direction suggested by news is probably going to go in the opposite direction.

What is important is how markets react to news, not how you think they should react. Put another way, the market is always right! Never fail to respect that fact.

Most newspapers that print Futures prices also carry a column which reports on markets for the previous day. They often suggest reasons for price moves that have little or nothing to do with reality. Smart money seldom moves after the news is out and newspapers don't report price movement, as they often should, in terms of what the emotion-driven and late-coming members of the public were doing.

FORMAL REPORTS

You should make a point of knowing when formal (usually government) reports are scheduled which could affect markets that you are trading or thinking of trading. When important reports are being released, don't be caught carrying bigger positions than you can readily afford, just in case price moves dramatically against you upon announcement of the news.

As a general rule, news announcements are expected to move markets in the direction of the trend. Therefore, with caution, be prepared to go into a trade or stay in a trade through an expected announcement of news, provided that there are valid signals to be in the market. Entering after an announcement can lead to the kind of knee-jerk reaction that puts you in at a bad price or at a level where the stop is no longer manageable.

It is particularly important to treat with maximum respect the quarterly hog and pig crop report (covering Live Hogs and Pork Bellies). Price frequently makes several limit moves afterwards, and not necessarily in the direction suggested by chart patterns. An informal rule of thumb for pig crop reports is that they often lead to major turns in the market when price is at a conspicuously high or low level.

The chart for February 1985 Pork Bellies shows violent reactions to quarterly pig crop reports.

Looking at this chart, you can see that you might have gone long before the March report, providing that you were well capitalized. A major reversal on the weekly chart had occurred at a support level (explained in Chapter 12) and a powerful buy signal was delivered before the report. Then price responded to the news with five limit moves!

For the June report, you could not reasonably have stayed in long positions through the report, with price already at a relatively high level above 80¢. The September report produced one limit move down that turned out to be an exhaustion move prior to a change of direction in the trend.

A list of important economic reports and activities for the coming week appears in *Barron's*. In addition, many brokerage houses print calendars for distribution to clients or will otherwise be able to provide information on the timing of agricultural and economic reports. Most monthly statistical reports on the U.S. economy are released between 8:30 and 10:00 a.m. Eastern Time, while other formal reports come out after the respective markets close.

While you are urged to treat all news reports with caution, they are not without value. On the contrary, markets cannot in the long run be moved without reasons that have a fundamental basis in the forces of supply and demand. If, for instance, there is very high demand for cotton and if carryover stocks from the previous year are low, price can go higher even in the face of a record crop. There are always conflicts such as these that sway

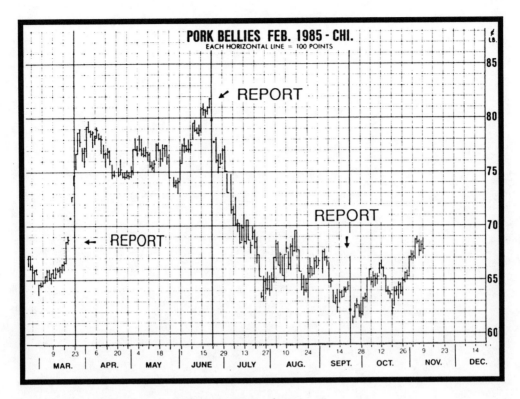

supply and demand, and you cannot ignore them.

On the other hand, our technical indicators will seldom let you down as the means of sorting out fundamental news, and they will seldom let you down badly when reports are announced. Nevertheless, it is a basic characteristic of Futures trading at all times that surprises can come out of the blue: one source of surprises can be the publication of reports.

Chapter 7

Trade With The Trend

Futures markets have their share of sayings. One of them is, "The trend is your friend." Although the saying sounds silly and the rhyme is offensive, the concept is valid. Ignoring the dominant trend is why many Futures traders lose money.

But how can a trend be identified?

Because one person's change of trend is merely a correction in a continuing trend for another, there has to be a standard working definition. Otherwise, the trend is likely to be interpreted in accordance with the emotions and other subjective variables, rather than in accordance with the discipline of a planned approach to trading.

DEFINING MARKET TRENDS

One of the most important components of the Wellspring System is the establishment of usable definitions of market trends. We use the *weekly* bar charts as the basis for designating the direction of markets.

A *rising or bull market* is defined as one having a succession of higher highs and higher lows on the weekly chart, forming an upward zigzag in the process.

A Rising Market

A *declining or bear market* has a succession of lower highs and lower lows.

A Declining Market

An *erratic market* has highs and lows occurring irregularly. A bull market becomes an erratic market when the preceding identifiable major low on the *weekly* chart is taken out or when price makes a clear top below the preceding major high. Similarly, a bear market becomes an erratic market when the preceding high is surpassed, or when price makes a clear low that is higher than a preceding low.

An erratic market may also be a sideways or trading range market, as discussed in Chapter 12, but only when price is confined in a relatively small range.

An Erratic Market

Using these definitions, buy only in rising markets; sell only in declining markets and avoid trading erratic markets.

The probabilities do not favor making money from trades taken against the major trend of the market. Sudden moves are likely to occur in the direction of the established trend. Contra-trend trades may therefore result in big losses that can outweigh many small profits. So avoid them!

Generally, you should also avoid taking trades in an erratic market, except when the requirements for an emerging bull market or an emerging bear market are fulfilled (described in Chapter 9). Occasionally, there will be circumstances where an apparently valid signal to trade in one direction will be followed by a signal to trade in the opposite direction (in symmetrical triangles, for instance, described in Chapter 12). However, the concept of trading only in the direction of the trend, as defined here by patterns of highs and lows on the weekly chart, should lead to consistent profits.

FOLLOWING THE TREND

The weekly chart for Soybean Oil clearly illustrates the principle of trading in the direction of an established trend, and of avoiding trades against the trend or in erratic markets.

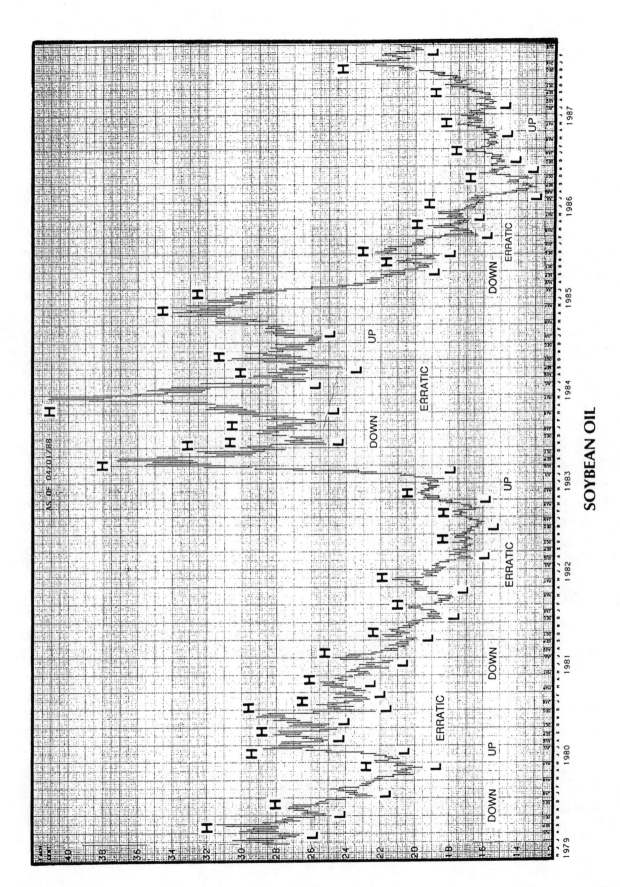

SOYBEAN OIL

43

Using our definitions for bull, bear and erratic markets, the Soybean Oil chart shows the following:

Trend	Weeks	Per Cent
Bull Market	75	22
Bear Market	145	42
Erratic Market	123	34
	345	100

Trading with the direction of the trend on the Soybean Oil chart would have led to consistent profits. Note the two huge trades where our definitions for identifying the trend delivered very clear signals. The buy at 18.5¢ went to 38¢ with barely a pause for breath, delivering a profit of $11,400 over about three months. The slide from 32¢ to 20¢ would have delivered a profit of $7,200. In addition to these very big profits, there were plenty of opportunities for steady bread-and-butter trades in the direction of the established trends.

The Soybean Oil chart also shows how important it is not to try to pick a top or bottom arbitrarily before the market has shown that it is ready to change direction. Trends take time to work themselves out; you can't hurry the process, as the approximately 85-week topping process in Soybean Oil demonstrates.

The most amateurish thing you can do is to try to pick a market top or bottom before its time in order to trade in the other direction. Contrary to what you might think, it is not admirable to pick an absolute top or bottom; it's more like foolish luck. Professionals trading Futures as a business wait to see a change of direction established with reasonable certainty. Then it is enough to take a piece of the profit — ideally a very large piece — out of the long stretch between the top and the bottom.

USING THE DAILY CHARTS

Although we primarily use the weekly charts to determine market trends, the daily charts may offer guidance when there is ambiguity in interpretation. Sometimes there may be divergent patterns between different contract months that could, for example, justify a short sale in a new-crop agricultural contract, despite strength in nearby old-crop contracts. Nevertheless, these differences do not detract materially from the general principle that you should be guided by trends defined by the nearest Futures contracts (which are the ones used to compile weekly charts).

When there are divergences in the patterns for different contract months, follow the rule of buying the strongest month and selling the weakest. As with other footprints left by traders, you should follow the leader.

SOME MARKETS HAVE LONG TRENDS, SOME DON'T

Financial markets, including the stock indexes, interest rates and currencies, often have very long-term trends lasting for several years because they tend to reflect macro-economic forces. Having no intrinsic cost of production, it is possible for price to head toward infinity, like the Japanese stock market of the 1980s, or toward zero, like the Mexican Peso in the early 1980s. Try to avoid being deluded by ideas about value when trading these markets. It's much safer and more reliable to believe the technical indicators.

Other Futures markets such as the meats, relatively seldom have very long trends, usually because of factors relating to producers' ability to respond to changes in supply and demand. For instance, breeders can significantly expand or contract the number of hogs within a year.

SLOW TRENDING MARKETS: DULL MARKETS MAKE MONEY!

The chart for March 1985 Sugar shows a steadily trending market that differs importantly from the kind of powerful and fast-moving markets that we are generally looking for.

The Sugar chart shows a trend par excellence, a dream trade that takes the idea of a trend to the ultimate. Sometimes you get a market that just keeps on going, day after day, week after week, slowly pumping out money like sausages coming out of a machine. The main characteristic of such a market is that the daily trading range is usually quite small and there is a steady pattern of price moving for a few days with the trend, then retracing or going sideways for a few days. But price keeps working slowly and surely, almost inevitably, in the direction of the established trend.

Many traders ignore these opportunities, thinking that the payoff comes too slowly. Possibly also many traders feel that such trades lack the excitement which they expect from trading Futures. Yet when faced with the ultra-high probability of these trades making money, the question to ask is: Do you want excitement or do you want to make money? If you want to make money with the least of worries, then these are the best of all trades.

Paradoxically, the slowness of such a relentless move is what virtually guarantees its continuation, as well as drastically lowers the chance of a violent or far-reaching retracement against the trend. A further advantage of these trades is that a market having low volatility usually requires less margin. So the gains as a percentage of capital invested are usually very favorable when considered over a period longer than just a few days.

If you had sold March 1985 Sugar in November of 1983 at 12.25¢, and stayed with the trade, you would not have been required to get out until October (11 months later), using our definitions of market trends as the basis for staying with the trade. (In reality, you would have traded one or more nearer contracts and rolled forward. Also, the Wellspring System would have had you in and out of the market a couple of times. But this doesn't negate the idea of staying with such a trade.)

The overall profit from 12.25¢ to 5¢ was 7.25¢ or $8,120, for a probable outlay of about $1,000 per contract in margin. This works out to 3 points or $40 per trading day. Each individual day would not make you rich. But you don't have to find many consecutive trades like this one to make a large amount of money. Start with one contract, and get up to a total of five contracts by the time you finally close out the trade, and you are on your way to multiplying the value of your account by several times.

Don't ignore these trades! Look for them in both rising and declining markets. Be prepared to get in and just ride them, adding positions when appropriate, if it suits you to do so. (Pyramiding is described in Chapter 22 on capital management.) These trades may look unglamorous (and are guaranteed to look unprofitable from your broker's perspective). But don't be fooled by a market that looks boring. Dullness can make an exciting amount of money!

CONCLUSION

The purpose in using our definitions for bull, bear and erratic markets is that they will result in consistency in trading. It doesn't matter if you miss some potential trades. When you have the means to enter a very high percentage of profitable ones, and especially when you have a system that will very seldom miss the really big profit trades, that is what counts in the long run. For it is even more important to avoid losses than it is to make profits!

All losses, even those that are paid for out of previously gained profits, give real money back to the market.

Chapter 8

Trading Formations Applied To The Weekly Charts

Trading formations were described in Chapter 4 as a means of entering markets when used with the daily charts. When applied to the weekly charts, they serve as a very important indicator. The rules for their application follow.

Rule 1. Directional Indicator

A trading formation on the weekly chart confirms the direction of the market and suggests that it will continue in that direction.

Rule 2. Turn Indicator

A trading formation on the weekly chart serves as a reliable indicator to signal completion of a retracement, or of a major turn in the market at long-term support or resistance.

Completion of a weekly trading formation often coincides with completion of a trading formation on the daily chart, although there may be one or two days difference in the timing of the completion.

Application of trading formation Rule 1, the three-day rule, should be treated with caution when applied to the weekly chart because it may bring price into the time frame for a retracement.

Rule 3. Closing Price Reversals

Trading formations differ in one important respect when applied to weekly charts, rather than to daily charts. It takes only a *single* closing price reversal bar (which includes a key reversal bar but does not include a high/low reversal, as described in Chapter 3) to indicate a likely market turn.

49

This does not mean that a closing price reversal on the weekly chart can be taken, on its own, as a signal to enter or close out a trade. As with other indicators, it must be coordinated with the trend of the market, and with trading formation and entry or liquidation signals on the daily chart. However, it is a reliable indicator of when a market may be ready to make a thrust in the direction of the reversal, whether to push the market further in the direction of the major trend or to make a retracement against the major trend. It is likely to occur at a major trendline or channel line (described in Chapter 10) or at an important level of support or resistance (described in Chapter 11).

All closing price reversals are significant. Even one not having a strong close suggests that traders, on balance, may be shifting their ideas about the direction of the market, at least for the near term. Key reversals on the weekly chart usually constitute a strong enough signal to enter the market right away, provided that the trend and other indicators confirm the trade.

The table below shows the record for 42 closing price reversals (excluding high/low reversals) on the weekly chart for Soybean Oil. When there was enough follow-through to trade in and out at a profit, it was assumed that the trade would have been profitable. No consideration was given to whether trading formations and entry signals coincided on the daily charts. In tabulating these results, closing price reversals which coincided with emerging trends (described in Chapter 9) were included with established trends.

	Profits	Losses	Total
Total closing price reversals	37 (55%)	30 (45%)	67
Closing price reversals *with* the trend	18 (64%)	10 (36%)	28
Closing price reversals *against* the trend or in erratic markets	19 (48%)	20 (52%)	39

Although 55% of all closing price reversals showed the potential for a profitable trade, 45% would have incurred losses. When only closing price reversals *with* the trend were taken, the proportion of profitable trades rose to 64% and the proportion of losses decreased to 36%, almost a 2:1 ratio. Obviously, the effect of trading with the trend is to increase net profits substantially.

The Soybean Oil chart was selected at random to illustrate the use of weekly closing price reversals as an indicator. These reversals will not always produce similar results. But you are likely to find, on balance, that they are an extremely valuable indicator when used in conjunction with other indicators.

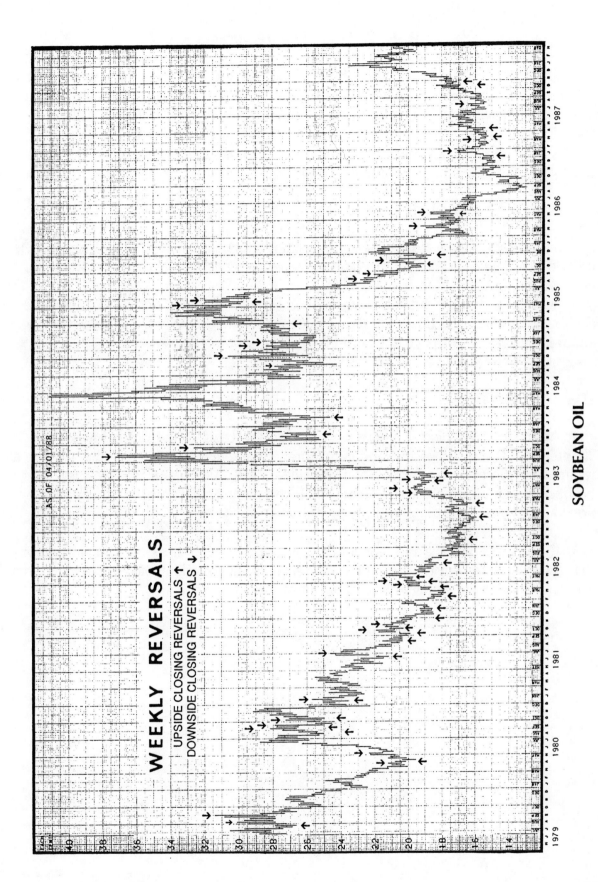

WEEKLY REVERSALS

UPSIDE CLOSING REVERSALS ↑
DOWNSIDE CLOSING REVERSALS ↓

AS OF 04/01/88

SOYBEAN OIL

51

Rule 4. High/Low Reversals

High/low reversals on the weekly chart do not have an equal weighting with closing price reversals. On their own, their reliability falls significantly below that for closing price reversals. However, they may be given equal weighting with closing price reversals, at your discretion, when they are substantial and occur at likely turning points.

Any reversals — high/low or closing price — repeated within a few bars are a particularly strong signal on the weekly chart.

Rule 5. Lindahl Formations and Double Reversals

While all trading formations on the weekly chart have validity when looking for markets to trade, pay particular attention to Lindahl formations and double reversals (which may also be part of a Lindahl formation).

When identifying a Lindahl formation, look for it to be completed within nine bars.

For double reversals, it is very desirable that the second reversal have a higher low when you are buying, or a lower high when selling.

ADVANCE ENTRY

In line with the concept of advance entry on the basis of the daily charts (Rule 3, Chapter 5), it is sometimes appropriate to enter a market during the week that you see a trading formation coming through on the weekly chart. Although trading formations on the weekly chart are a powerful indicator, their completion can come after the market has moved more than necessary to justify an entry.

In the next chapter, we discuss identifying how a new trend starts. Trading formations on the weekly chart provide one of the most reliable means of identifying the market turns that contribute to the larger picture of which markets to trade.

Chapter 9

How A New Trend Starts

You have been warned never to try to pick tops and bottoms of markets before their time. This does not means, though, that you should hesitate to enter a market at the earliest possible moment once it shows real signs of changing direction. Indeed, you should look to get into a new trend as soon as the probabilities favor doing so, in order to accomplish the objective of buying low and selling high.

How, then, can new trends be recognized?

The answer follows from our definition of bull and bear markets in Chapter 7. A bull market is indicated by a pattern on the *weekly* chart that begins with one higher high and one higher low (in that order or the reverse). Similarly, a bear market begins with one lower high and one lower low (or vice versa).

Given these definitions, we now apply them to finding new trends on the weekly charts. The beginning of the zigzag that defines a bull market begins with a W; the beginning of the zigzag that defines a bear market begins with an M. Each of them has two variants, depending on whether initial highs or lows occur first.

W-FORMATIONS FOR EMERGING BULL MARKETS

W-Formation: Initial Higher High

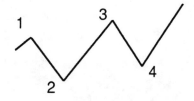

When the *higher high* comes first, look for the following:

1. The low at (2) is assumed to be the bottom of the market after the high at (3) has exceeded the previous high on the weekly chart at (1).

2. After the higher high at (3) is in place, expect a retracement and look for a bottom to form at (4).

3. Enter a trade on the long side at (4) on completion of a clear trading formation on the *daily* chart. Ideally, this signal should be accompanied by a trading formation on the weekly chart (described in Chapter 8).

4. Don't press the market for your entry if the signals are less than completely clear.

    The retracement from (3) to (4) may last for several weeks and give up 50% to almost 100% of the price gain between (2) and (3). Often this retracement sets up a pattern of lower highs and lower lows on the *daily* chart, but that does not negate the potential for a change in the major trend.

5. The low at (4) must go no lower than the low at (2). (Generally the second low will be higher than the first one. However, it is remarkable how often lows occur at almost exactly the same level.)

    A *lower low* invalidates a W-Formation. A *close* lower than (2) confirms the downward pressure on the market, which is likely to continue.

6. After entering a long position in accordance with the above, expect the next high to be above (3).

    Failure to move above (3) negates the emerging bull market. You may not know that it's failing until later. But you are likely to get a signal to liquidate the trade if it is going to stall out (described in Chapter 13, Stops and Liquidation of Trades). If you get out prematurely, you can always take the next signal to go long, provided that the emerging bull market has not been negated.

W-Formation: Initial Higher Low

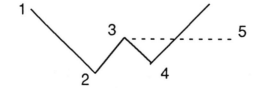

When the *higher low* comes first, modify the approach as follows:

1. Look for a clear low at (4) that goes no lower than (2).

2. Enter a long position at (5) when there is a signal from a trading formation on the *daily* chart that coincides with the break above (3).

   After price has broken out above (3), in the case of either an initial higher high or an initial higher low, there may be a retracement back to the breakout level. Don't be discouraged; this is normal. But you shouldn't wait to enter the market until this retracement comes (as some books recommend). Some of the best trades never retrace, but you never tell in advance whether they will or not.

M-FORMATIONS FOR EMERGING BEAR MARKETS

The theory of entering trades at the beginning of a bear market is essentially the same as for an emerging bull market, only upside down — an M instead of a W.

M-Formation: Initial Lower Low

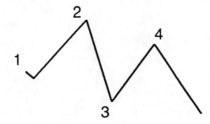

When the *lower low* comes first, look for the following:

1. The high at (2) is assumed to be the top of the market after the low at (3) has exceeded the previous low on the weekly chart at (1).

2. After the lower low at (3) is in place, expect a retracement and look for a top to form at (4).

3. Enter a trade on the short side at (4) on completion of a clear trading formation on the *daily* chart. Ideally, this signal should be accompanied by a trading formation on the *weekly* chart (described in Chapter 8).

4. Don't press the market for your entry if the signals are less than completely clear.

The retracement from (3) to (4) may last for several weeks and give up 50% to almost 100% of the decline in price between (2) and (3).

A bear market may begin more rapidly than a bull market, particularly if the market is extremely over-bought. However, there is also a greater risk of being whipsawed when trying to catch the beginning of a bear market. Therefore, you should be very careful to check that you have most indicators confirming your entry and pay extra heed to indicators negating the trade. In particular, avoid trying to pick the beginning of a bear market while any obvious uptrend lines remain unbroken. (See Chapter 10, Trendlines.)

5. After entering a short position in accordance with the above, expect the next low to be below (3).

Failure to move below (3) negates the emerging bear market. You may not know that it's failing until later. But in any case you are unlikely to go far wrong by watching for a signal to liquidate and acting on it immediately if one comes through. You may be knocked out of some good trades prematurely, but you will also protect yourself from the risk of profits turning to bad losses.

M-Formation: Initial Lower High

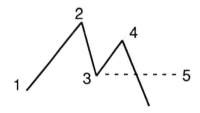

When the *lower high* comes first, modify the approach as follows:

1. Look for a clear high at (4) that goes no higher than (2).

2. Enter a short position at (5) when there is a signal from a trading formation on the *daily* chart that coincides with a break below (3).

As with emerging bull markets, there may be a retracement back to the breakdown level. This does not negate the validity of the breakdown. But these retracements can be nerve-wracking. The remedy for anxiety is to know that trades taken at the potential beginning of a bear market can be so hugely profitable that, on balance, the profits will far outweigh the losses. Just never enter a bigger position than you can afford if the trade doesn't work — either in emotional or financial capital.

W AND M-FORMATIONS ILLUSTRATED

By returning to the weekly chart for Soybean Oil (page 59), we can bring together the three indicators discussed in Chapters 7, 8 and 9 — the definition of bull and bear markets, the application of trading formations to the weekly charts, and M and W-Formations. Applied jointly, they can signal entries to major trades.

The first trade, Buy (1), came out of a lopsided W with an initial higher low as price moved rapidly up from the 20¢ level. There was a strong buy signal on the basis of the three-day rule applied to the weekly chart, but this was as far as price went initially before retracing 50% of the gain. Then a Lindahl buy formation came through in seven bars and before the breakout. Note how the Lindahl formation itself comprises most of the W-Formation.

Entry on completion of the Lindahl formation would have gotten you in at about 21.6¢. This compares with 22.4¢, where the entry would normally be on the basis of a breakout from a W-Formation having an initial higher low. This trade shows how profitable it can be to get into a trade right away when a very powerful signal is delivered. It also shows how different signals to enter a trade may come through at slightly different times. Here entry on completion of the Lindahl formation on the weekly chart could be made on the assumption that the W-formation breakout would also come through.

The second W-Formation that delivered a signal, Buy (2), didn't work. It had all the characteristics of a W-Formation with an initial higher high, seemingly confirmed with a good weekly closing price reversal. But the market just wasn't ready to make its turn. However, a stop-loss below the bottom of the weekly reversal bar would have resulted in a loss of only about 75 points, which is insignificant in the overall scheme of things.

Buy (2) provides a good example of how you can and must enter trades when all the signals are right to do so. You recognize that some trades having excellent signals won't work. But the Soybean Oil chart also shows that second-guessing first class signals will result in missing the best opportunities.

The third W-Formation marked the beginning of one of the biggest ever moves in Soybean Oil. The weekly upside reversal signaling Buy (3a) delivered an entry signal just 80 points above the low for the bear market. In addition, this reversal constituted a double reversal and completion of a Lindahl buy formation in nine bars.

You would probably have been in and out of the market several times during the consolidation which lasted 13 weeks below the 20¢ level. This consolidation was very turbulent, as the bars on the weekly chart show: three strong upside reversals and three strong downside reversals. Trading with the trend by taking trades only in conjunction with the upside reversals would not, however, have lost you money except, possibly, for a very small loss on the second reversal. This would have happened if you liquidated after completion of the weekly reversal against the trade. Trading against the trend by taking the first downside reversal, a high/low reversal, would have lost money, although the subsequent two would have delivered small profits.

This consolidation demonstrates the importance of approaching markets with a mindset of trading only with the major trend. Having this mindset would prevent you from being mentally sidetracked from re-entering the market when a first-rate buy signal finally came through. The entry at Buy (3b) signaled strongly with a key reversal that there should be a major move up.

Note that there was never any reason to consider liquidating a long position entered at about 19.3¢ until completion of the weekly downside reversal at 33¢. It is true that the top was above 37¢. But you should normally wait for a signal to exit because attempts to pick market tops arbitrarily are almost always premature.

Buy (4) shows a potential entry that was negated by the principles of W-Formations. The second low violated the W pattern; consequently, you would have had to look for other compelling reasons to buy. An entry could be justified by the convincing size of the weekly upside reversal, which occurred at the same approximate level as the previous low, as well as by the fact that there was no weekly close below the preceding low.

The signal at Buy (5) coincided with a rather ragged W-Formation. Nevertheless, it was identifiable as one having a higher high than the spikes several weeks earlier. Notice the huge high/low reversal that occurred at Buy (5), with a very small down bar but a very large up bar.

The entry at Sell (1) is questionable because of the raggedness of the M-Formation. Since there was almost a closing price reversal, it is virtually certain that there would have been a strong trading formation on the daily chart to signal an entry. The trade might otherwise have been taken when a Lindahl sell signal came through on the weekly chart three weeks later.

There were no such difficulties with an entry at Sell (2), where the major trend and the M-Formation were both very clear and there was a good downside reversal.

The signal at Sell (3) is particularly worth noting as an example of how to handle an emerging bear market at the end of a huge bull market, when price action may be extremely volatile.

You will see a massive M-Formation that formed over a period of almost 18 months, as well as an even larger head and shoulders pattern, discussed at the end of this chapter. Within the area of the second high of the huge M, you might have had great difficulty finding a place to enter because of the volatility of the market. It lasted for a full eight weeks after the top, before a convincing signal came through. This consisted of a double reversal, which was also the *second* Lindahl sell formation made during the topping process. A very compressed M-Formation was completed within this period as well, further suggesting a high probability of a top being securely in place.

After these multiple signals suggesting a top were delivered, the market proceeded to drop like a stone. This action demonstrates the huge potential for a trade entered at the beginning of a bear market. But it also demonstrates that you must be extremely patient

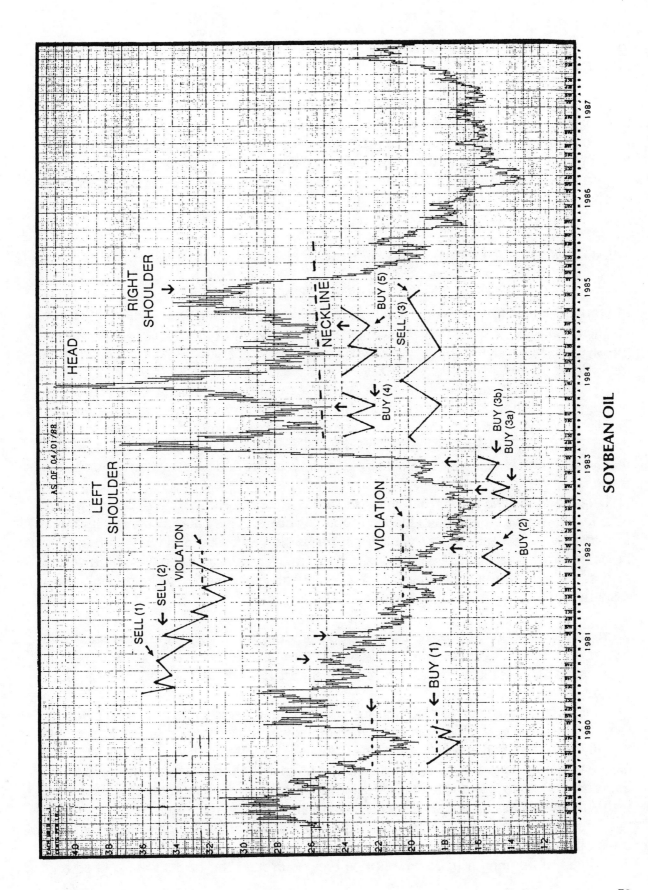

SOYBEAN OIL

in assembling the evidence to justify proceeding with such a trade. Remember the adage, "Bull markets die hard!"

M and W-Formations are invaluable for getting into big moves as early as it is realistic to trade a market turn. Since bull and bear markets start relatively infrequently and can last a long time, you will be looking to enter a trade in the direction of an established trend far more often. But Ms and Ws often offer the chance to get in on the ground floor (or the top floor) of huge trades just as they are starting. So they are well worth watching for — and watching patiently for the right time to enter.

HEAD AND SHOULDERS, AND REVERSE HEAD AND SHOULDERS

The head and shoulders formation is related to M-Formations. Essentially, it is a triple top formation, while it takes only two tops to qualify an M-Formation. Each of the three tops generally comprises a period of congestion. The weekly Soybean Oil chart shows a massive head and shoulders formation which developed over a two-year period between mid-1983 and mid-1985.

To make a head and shoulders formation, price makes a high once and backs away, making the left shoulder. It then makes a higher high and backs away, making the head. Finally, it makes a third high that is lower than the middle one and, ideally, lower than the first one, although this is not a mandatory requirement. Preferably, this pattern should be relatively symmetrical; undue raggedness suggests volatility and a lack of conviction by big traders.

The theory behind this formation is that it indicates total exhaustion of buying power after a major move up and an extended topping process. This pattern shares with other formations the tendency to be significant in proportion to its size and the length of time in the making. A valid head and shoulders can form over a few years on a long-term chart or it can develop on a daily chart. Often a Lindahl sell formation will also look like a miniature head and shoulders formation.

A popular theory of how to enter a trade on completion of a head and shoulders formation states that you sell when price breaks through the "neckline" (see Soybean Oil chart, page 59). There are problems with this theory that you should know about, given its popularity.

First, it can be difficult to enter a trade when there is a stampede of people all trying to trade the same way. The Soybean Oil chart shows that the market went into free fall and plunged straight through the neckline. Second, it is often difficult to know where to draw a neckline that makes sense. The neckline on the Oil chart has two points of contact but is actually quite arbitrary. Third, it can be extremely difficult to enter at the neckline with a manageable stop and the popularity of doing so sometimes leads to traps — false breakouts that suck in the unwary. Consequently, the risk of a rebound is greater than it is with breaks out of most other congestion patterns.

Instead of entering a trade when price breaks through the neckline of a head and shoulders formation, we look to enter as the market is turning at the right shoulder. As with any move, we try to get in at the start rather than enter after it has already gone so far that there is a high risk of it retracing suddenly from an overbought or oversold condition. The entry at the turn of the right shoulder was discussed earlier in the chapter as Sell (3).

A reverse head and shoulders is the same thing as a head and shoulders pattern, only upside down, and is related to W-Formations. It therefore serves to give advance notice of a potentially big trade on the long side.

The weekly Gold chart and the cash Gold chart in Chapter 11 (pages 75 and 77) provide additional illustrations of head and shoulders, and reverse head and shoulders formations.

Chapters 7, 8 and 9 have described how to identify and use existing major trends and emerging new trends. Chapters 10, 11 and 12 describe several indicators that relate the fluctuation of markets, the continuation of trends and their turning points.

Chapter 10

Trendlines, Linear Retracement And Channel Lines

TRENDLINES AND LINEAR RETRACEMENT

A trendline connects *lows* in a rising market and *highs* in a declining market. Price is expected to move in zigzags or waves away from the trendline in the established direction. Then it is expected to retrace back in the direction of the trendline before starting the next outward wave in the established direction. Hence, linear retracement. Another way of looking at the fluctuations of price against a trendline is to compare it with the way that a sailboat might tack backwards and forwards while maintaining a steady overall direction along a shoreline.

Trendlines help to identify markets to trade by showing their direction and momentum. They provide guidance in forecasting how far price might retrace, and when and where price might start to advance again.

Drawing trendlines is an art, not a science. Sometimes you have to draw them as best you can, which may involve fudging a line through the middle of bars rather than through their tips, or by connecting with a close rather than with the end of a bar. Some people try to join all possible highs or lows and end up with so many lines that the overall result is useless.

A trendline may be short-term, connecting prices over just a few days or weeks. Particularly when a short-term trendline is steep, it will generally not remain unbroken for long. On the other hand, a very long-term trendline on a weekly or monthly chart may connect prices over many months or even years.

You can start a tentative trendline as soon as two highs or two lows are clearly established. However, the validity of the trendline will be confirmed only when price returns to a third point on or near the trendline and rebounds from it. If the market's rate of change accelerates, it may be necessary to draw a steeper trendline, although doing so would not invalidate an earlier one, particularly if it has three points of contact.

Five principles for using trendlines are described below. The weekly chart for the D-Mark, the daily chart for the December 1985 D-Mark and the daily chart for April 1987 Gold are used for illustration.

1. The validity of trendlines increases in proportion to the length of time between connecting highs or lows, thus generally making trendlines on weekly charts much more significant than those on daily charts.

    You can see from the weekly chart for the D-Mark that just four very long major trends (marked with Roman numerals) were established over a period of more than ten years. (There were, of course, many intermediate trends and shorter trends that are not marked.)

    Note that trendline III-IV was twice re-drawn steeper. The lines connecting A - C and C - D were superseded by a trendline that began by connecting D - E. You will also see how price moved up through trendline IX-X without even pausing, although it had been in force for nine months.

    The point of this principle is to show that markets can keep on going in an established direction, in the very big picture, for an exceedingly long time. It is all too easy to be sidetracked from the big picture by looking at daily charts, and thus be tempted into trades against the overall direction of the market.

2. Price can be expected to retrace on weekly charts to a long-standing trendline, which becomes a target, to stop at or near it, and then to continue in the direction of the established trend.

    This principle follows from the first one. A long-standing trendline is seen by traders as a marker-buoy. On the other hand, a very steep trendline is likely to result from a temporary acceleration in price, rather than a change in the overall momentum of the market. You often see steep, short-term trends on daily charts.

3. The entry to a potential major trade is signaled by a trading formation on the *daily* chart occurring when price has retraced to a point at or near a trendline on the *weekly* chart. Ideally, the trading formation on the daily chart will also be contained within a trading formation on the weekly chart; for example, a weekly reversal.

    Once trendline III-IV was redrawn to connect D and E, it was virtually certain that the high/low reversal at F signaled the entry to a major trade. Trendline V-VI shows textbook turns at K, M and O. The turns at I, J and L show how price can move through a trendline without negating its validity.

4. A major new trend in the opposite direction is signaled when price crosses a long-term trendline on the *weekly* chart, provided that:

International Monetary Market
Weekly High, Low-Friday Close
Nearest Futures Contract

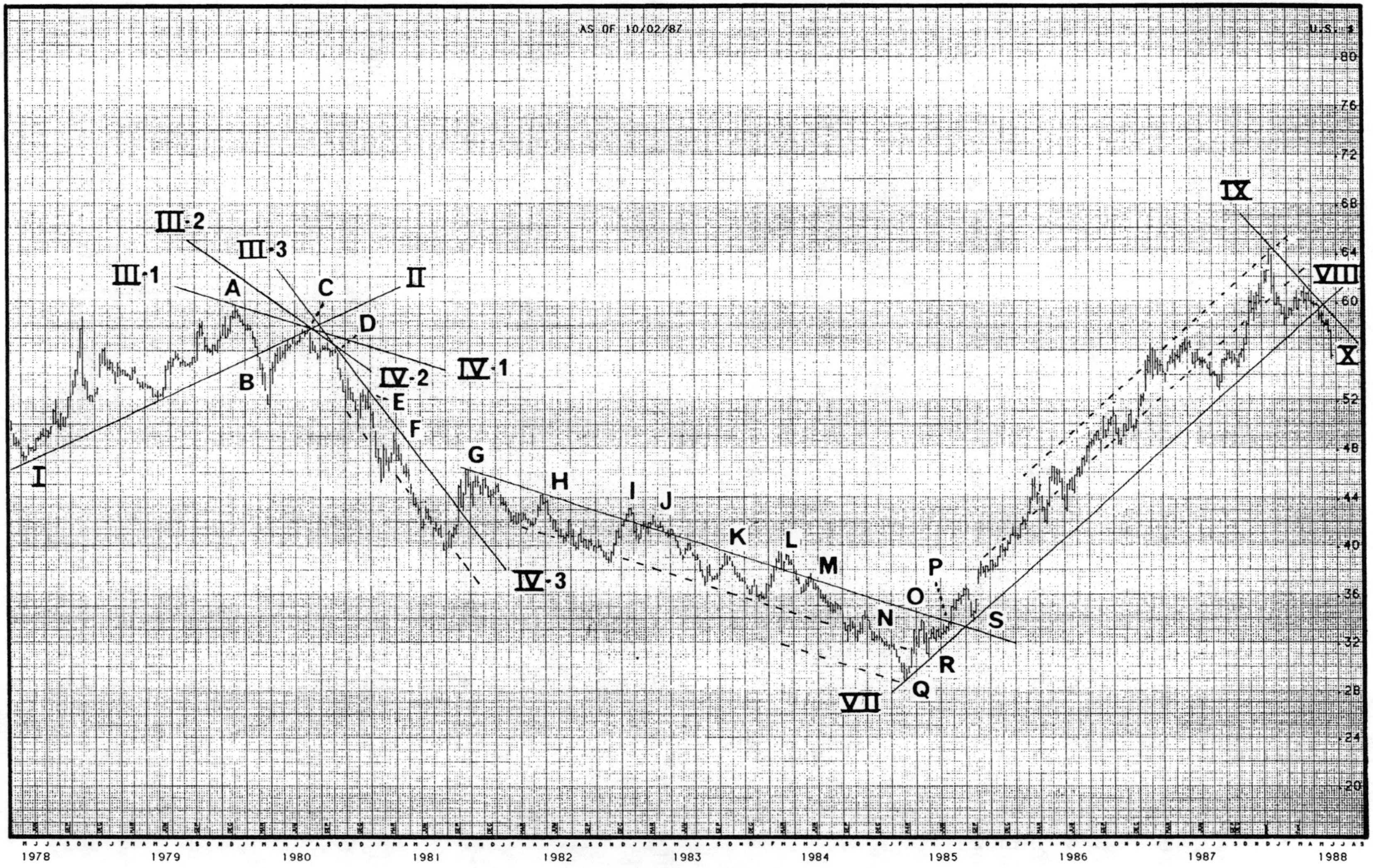

AS OF 10/02/87

DEUTSCHE MARK

a)   there is a valid W or M-Formation in force; and

b)   there is a pronounced acceleration as price crosses the trendline.

The breakout at P fulfilled these requirements and a new trend was confirmed accordingly. In contrast, the crossover at J coincided with an emerging W-Formation but there was minimal acceleration in price.

The Wellspring System rejects a popular belief about price crossing long-term trendlines. It is widely held that a crossover of such a trendline, in itself, signals a trade in the direction of the crossover. According to this view, the crossover of trendline I-II at B would be a valid sell signal. While this particular signal would have been profitable, for us there was no trade. Price came straight off a higher high without stopping and the market was already technically oversold by the time price reached the trendline. Under such circumstances, a sudden rebound can occur at any time, as did happen when the market turned violently for its rally up to C.

It is more valuable to pass the entry at B, as well as to pass the similar potential entries at I, J and L. Not only did these last three fail to work as buy signals, but the bullish mindset that taking them might have encouraged could have resulted in missing the opportunities to enter profitable short positions.

If you miss an entry when price crosses a long-term trendline and the conditions of Principle 4 are met (as at P), be patient about waiting for the next opportunity. There is almost always another good place to enter, as at S when price returned to the trendline to make a third contact. Alternatively, look for an entry on the daily chart in accordance with the trend continuation rule (described in Chapter 4).

5(a) Price crossing a short-term trendline on the *daily* chart can confirm a signal to enter a trade.

This principle does not mean that trading formations must be validated by the additional requirement of price crossing a short-term trendline. However, a crossover can resolve ambiguity in favor of taking a trade when price has been retracing or consolidating for some time and when the signals from trading formations are weak.

The chart for April 1987 Gold shows short-term trendlines used with trading formations both to enter new positions and to liquidate open positions (Principle 5(b)). During the period covered by this chart, Gold was in a bull market, as defined by a succession of higher highs and higher lows on the weekly chart. Therefore, we would take trades only on the long side.

The search for a new entry on the long side, as price retraced from the $450 level,

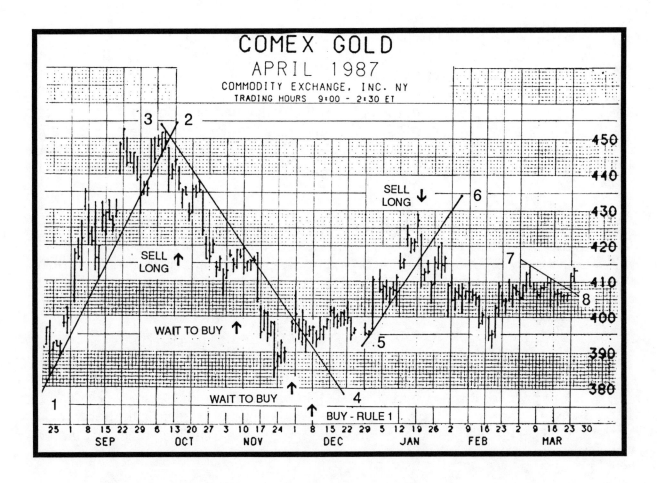

involved waiting for a trading formation to be completed. While waiting, an identifiable high formed on October 23 which permitted trendline 3-4 to be drawn, thus suggesting that at least a short-term downtrend had been established. Although there were two clear buy signals in November on the basis of trading formations, note that price did not break out of its short-term downtrend until it closed convincingly over the downtrend line. After doing so, it proceeded to work its way higher, reversing the short-term downtrend.

Short-term trendlines can often be drawn across the tops or bottoms of quite small retracements and congestion areas. As with trendline 3-4 on the Gold chart, you can never be certain when a small retracement might turn into something bigger. It is therefore useful to draw short-term trendlines across such small chart patterns, as in the case of trendline 7-8.

The price action relating to trendline 7-8 is particularly interesting. There was a buy signal on Friday, March 20 after five consecutive closes in the upper half of the range. Because the daily range was small, you might have had doubts about entering the market in view of the existence of the trendline. The following Monday the price gapped over the downtrend line and was on its way to a major move up. Had you waited to enter until Monday, you would have entered at a higher price. But you would have done so after any ambiguity about resumption of the bull market had been resolved by the gap over the trendline.

5(b) Price crossing a short-term trendline on the *daily* chart and closing in the top or bottom 25% of the day's range *against* the trade is a signal to liquidate. You may, however, exercise discretion about liquidating the trade if the day's range lacks power and if price merely tests into a gap. (See also Chapter 13, Stops and Liquidation of Trades.)

You might initially have tried to draw a trendline on the December 1985 D-mark chart even steeper than 1-2. However, there was no satisfactory second point of contact until the small retracement at the beginning of April was completed. Even if you had drawn a steeper trendline, you should not have liquidated long positions on this first retracement because of the support suggested by the gap (described further in Chapter 11).

Once a clear correction low was in place, there was no doubt about where to draw a short-term trendline. Subsequently, you should have gotten out of the market before price went through trendline 1-2, in accordance with Liquidation Rule 3(a) (price gaps against the trade, Chapter 13). Any doubt about staying in the trade would have been demolished by price smashing through the trendline and closing at the bottom.

Trendlines 3-4 and 5-6 show how liquidating a trade when price closes forcefully through a trendline serves to protect profits or to minimize losses. Remember that we don't attempt to buy at absolute bottoms or to sell at absolute tops: it is enough to take a major piece out of the middle of a move. Covering long positions on the low close below trendline 3-4 would have gotten you out 150 points from the top. Never mind! You banked 250 points or $3,125. Re-entering with the next buy signal on August 8 and getting out on September 2, when price crossed trendline 5-6, would have banked 30 points or $375. An additional entry might have been taken on September 4, although the pattern of lower highs showing distribution, the feeble action on the Rule 2 entry day and proximity to the channel line (discussed at the end of this chapter) could have deterred you from taking the trade. If you did take it, the exit would have been on Friday two days later, with a loss of 70 points or $875. In the overall scheme of things, such a loss is to be regarded as a normal cost of doing business. The important point is that timely liquidation of long positions, aided by trendlines, would have allowed you to enter the next long position at about .3480, on the rebound from the trendline.

The daily chart for April 1987 Gold (page 67) also shows the use of trendlines for liquidating trades.

You would disregard the crossover of trendline 1-2 intra-day on September 29 with the close on the trendline, as well as the insignificant day on October 1, when price closed just under the trendline. The next crossover involved a clear close below the trendline after a small double top, as well as a second weekly reversal. However, it took a couple of days more before there was a low close and the gap was filled on a closing basis and, in addition, price closed in the bottom 25% of the day's range, thereby dictating mandatory liquidation of long positions on October 14. On the other hand, it took only one day of smashing down to require liquidation of long positions after price crossed trendline 5-6 and also left an island behind on January 20.

Trendline 5-6 also shows how there can be considerable arbitrariness in drawing trendlines, particularly in the short term. This line was drawn where it is partly

because it has an incline comparable with the one for trendline 1-2. It was assumed that the advance might travel at the same approximate speed as the last one.

CHANNEL LINES

Channel lines on both weekly and daily charts serve as tentative boundary lines for the peaks or valleys of price waves that start at or near a long-term or intermediate-term trendline.

Once you have established a trendline that you expect to last for some time, you can draw a channel line parallel with a trendline. Start if off the high that comes between the two lows marking the first important wave up. Or off the low that comes between the two highs marking the first important wave down.

The weekly D-Mark chart (page 65) shows how price can move in waves that are generally confined within a channel. After the final drawing of downtrend line III-IV, a channel line drawn off the first prominent low established a rough and ready boundary for subsequent fluctuations away from the trendline. The channel line drawn parallel with trendline V-VI was more effective, defining a channel for almost three years.

An even more striking example of the precision with which channel lines can work is shown on the December 1985 D-Mark chart (page 69). The tentative trend and channel lines were drawn once the high at the end of April and the low in early May were both in place.

Two months after the channel line was drawn, price stopped just 50 points short of it on July 18 and made a big key reversal, filling a gap on a closing basis in the process. (Our procedure for liquidating trades calls for covering long positions on this action, although you could have re-entered two days later on the upside reversal.) Two weeks later, price went within 20 points of the channel line and was turned away by it, making a substantial high/low reversal. This action led to a signal to liquidate long positions in accordance with price crossing the short-term trendline, as already discussed.

On August 9 a powerful buy signal at .3615 coincided with a strong upside weekly reversal. The fact that price had turned back twice near the channel line does not mean that such a trade should be avoided. Rather, after entering a trade near a channel line, watch to see whether price accelerates, thereby suggesting a breakthrough, or whether it falters, thereby suggesting that the line will turn price back. In the case of the D-Mark, price action near the channel line became obviously labored. A move to within 10 points of the channel line in late August ended with a closing price reversal, which set the stage for a significant retracement back to the major uptrend line.

There were several options for liquidating a long position on the failure at the channel line. You could have liquidated on the basis of the closing reversal itself, given its failure at the channel line and a close in the bottom 25% of the day's range. Alternatively, you could have entered an ordinary stop, rather than a close only stop (described in Chapter 13, Stop Rule 5), at about .3625 — under the trendline and under the most recent small spike. This would have gotten you out about 50 points earlier than waiting for the mandatory exit on the low close below the trendline.

When price accelerates through a channel line, there is a high probability of it continuing and of eventually going the same distance further as the width of the original channel.

Once price goes strongly through a channel line, draw a new line parallel with the first one, making the new channel the same width as the first one. The original channel line is then expected to serve as the trendline for the new channel.

Note on the weekly D-mark chart how price fell through the channel line to make a low at Q, reaching almost double the distance between the trendline and the first channel line. You can also see how double channel lines parallel with trendline VII-VIII served to contain price fluctuations. After price struggled over the top of the original channel line, also shown on the daily D-Mark chart, this line developed the supportive characteristics of a new trendline.

In conclusion, you must draw trendlines and channel lines on your charts. Estimating them by a casual glance doesn't show you what other traders are seeing. Just don't draw so many lines as to cause more clutter than clarification!

Chapter 11

Support And Resistance

The previous chapter discussed how price can be expected to move in zigzags or waves while maintaining an overall direction, like a sailboat tacking back and forth. Markets move from a turning point toward a target, where they can be expected to turn, retrace some of the recent move, then turn again in the main direction, and so on.

Chapter 10 looked at the diagonal movement of markets in relation to both a time base and a price base. This chapter looks at price targets and turning points from a horizontal perspective, without reference to time expectations. When price goes down, it is expected to reach toward a support level and probably turn up there. When price goes up, it is expected to reach toward a resistance level and probably turn down there.

HIGHS AND LOWS AS SUPPORT AND RESISTANCE

All markets are influenced by psychology. We discussed in Chapter 6 how traders are influenced by historically high and low prices. The same kind of thinking affects most people. Almost everyone talks about bargains they've found or high prices at which they have been able to sell. The price of haircuts or houses, stamp collections or stocks, paintings by Goya or Van Gogh are all subject to perceptions of being cheap or expensive. One of the most important influences on these perceptions is our use of yardsticks to measure value.

As an example, if Gold is $5 higher than yesterday, today it looks perceptibly more expensive. But if you had bought Gold in 1960 at $35, a $5 increase would not make you feel richer. Or if you had bought gold at $800, a $5 increase would not decrease your pain. Price, therefore, looks high or low relative to the yardstick of personal experience that each individual uses to measure it. The weekly Gold chart on page 75 shows how price seems to have been affected by the psychology of traders seeing price revisit old highs and lows.

We draw on both the weekly and daily charts horizontal dashed lines forward from previous highs and lows to indicate the level future advances and declines may aim for and where they may turn. On the daily charts we also draw horizontal lines at the level of the contract high and low, even if the price action on the chart does not include these levels. They represent the extremity of what has been considered high and low for that particular contract, and they assume increasing importance the longer they have held.

After the big runup in Gold over $800 in January 1980, a secondary high was made three weeks later at $725. After plunging to $450, Gold worked its way back up and briefly touched the $725 level again in September. Anyone who had bought high in early 1980 had a brief chance to recoup much of the loss. On the other hand, those who had bought on the decline would be able to make a hefty profit by selling in the $700 range. Traders interested in selling short would also welcome the opportunity to sell at a known high level in the hope that price would return to $450.

A combination of history and psychology resulted in an almost exact repeat of a high at $725 and another low at $450 several months later. Although the second low was not long lasting, it was an important one from which a $100 rally developed.

This process was repeated subsequently with new parameters for perceived high and low prices. A low at just under $300 occurred in 1982. The psychology of buyers hunting for a bargain came into play again when price returned to that level three years later. Similarly, once the $500 level became established as a prominent high in 1983, sellers were again able to overcome the force of buyers when the price returned there almost five years later.

Thus, major highs function as major resistance and major lows function as major support. Once reached, a major support or resistance level is expected to become a turning point for price to set out on a long journey back to the opposite extremity. No matter how long it may take, traders know where these long-term levels of support and resistance exist and they place their money accordingly. Markets don't forget!

It can readily be seen that markets establish levels, like levels in a high-rise building, within which prices fluctuate. This happens as a result of two factors already discussed in part.

In a rising market, those wanting to get in at a perceived good price before price goes higher become buyers on dips toward the previous resistance level. Also buying on dips toward this level — now the new support level — are traders on the short side wanting to cut losses before they get bigger. Similarly, in a declining market, sellers wanting to get in at a perceived good price before it goes lower sell on rallies toward the previous support level. Traders on the long side wanting to cut losses sell on rallies toward this level — now the new resistance level.

The face-off between buyers and sellers having conflicting reasons to trade and differing views on the direction of the market often results in periods when markets are in relative equilibrium, which shows up on charts as congestion areas. Sometimes, however, markets can continue in a general sideways direction for weeks, months or years when there is a general consensus that overall supply and demand are roughly in balance.

The process of how price ceilings become price floors — and how floors become ceilings — can be explained by looking further at Gold.

74

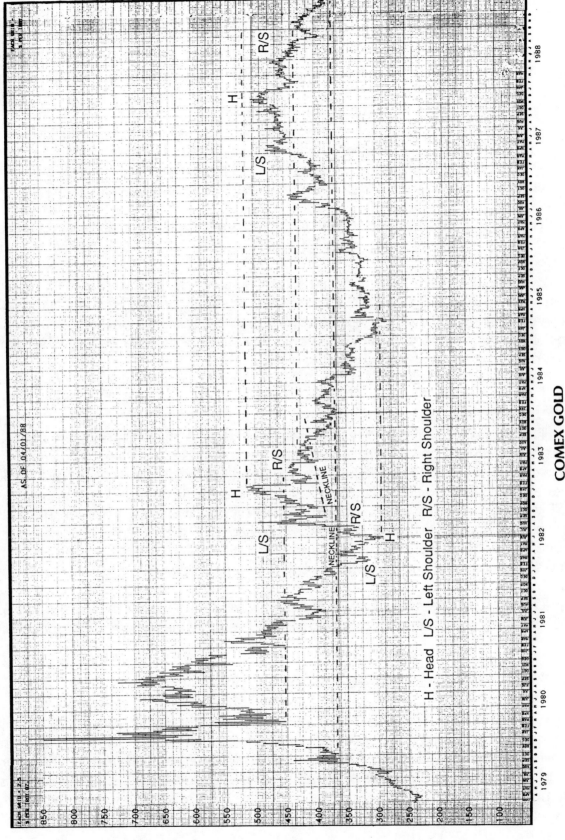

Commodity Exchange, Inc.
Weekly High, Low-Friday Close
Nearest Futures Contract

AS OF 04/01/88

H - Head   L/S - Left Shoulder   R/S - Right Shoulder

COMEX GOLD

The weekly Gold chart shows a dashed line right across the chart at the $360 level. It started at a low in 1979 which was prominent in the runup to $800 (although not clearly shown on this chart). This level offered only minor support for six weeks on the way down in 1982, but price stopped at $360 twice when it attempted to rally back up. Then in 1984, $360 provided support for almost six months before price broke through. After this break, price remained below the $360 ceiling for three years.

The chart for cash Gold during 1985 and 1986 shows in detail essentially what you would see if you smoothed the weekly bar chart. In January 1986, price rallied up to the $360 level and backed away almost as fast as it got there. It spent two weeks testing the under side and then fell to the $330 level, which had provided resistance for three months immediately prior to the surge to $360.

The daily chart for December 1986 Gold covers the same period as the chart for cash Gold. It shows the day-to-day reaction of traders to all market forces, including important support and resistance levels.

Because the price of Futures includes carrying charges, there are variations in chart patterns compared with the cash chart. The earlier period shows Futures trading much higher relative to cash, with the gap narrowing toward July. Although the November high in the cash price exceeded its September high, the opposite occurred in the December contract because of decreasing carrying charges.

Note the proximity in price of the three lows occurring in December, April and June on the Futures chart. Traders are influenced not only by cash prices, but also by the Futures contracts that they are trading.

The congestion area lasting approximately two weeks at the high in January shows the concept of support and resistance working on a smaller scale. The huge one-day rally above $390 in December 1986 Futures, corresponding to the $360 level in cash, looked like a terminal aberration. Nonetheless, buyers and sellers faced off for two weeks following this surge, in a price range bounded by support at $370 and resistance at $380. To test whether this two-week congestion area had truly resolved the opposing views of value in Gold, the market returned twice, in February and March, to roughly the $370 level and found that what had previously been temporary support had now become impenetrable resistance.

The same processes that produce the support and resistance levels discussed here also work at finer gradations on the daily charts, as well as in the microcosm of intra-day charts.

GAPS AS SUPPORT AND RESISTANCE

As discussed in Chapter 3, gaps can be a reliable indicator of important buying or selling power. When a gap occurs as part of a trading formation, it suggests that a worthwhile move may develop. When a breakaway gap occurs on the breakout from a congestion area or trading range, or over a major trendline on the weekly or daily chart, it suggests a stampede of buying or selling. And when a runaway gap occurs in a market that is either skyrocketing or collapsing, it indicates a continuing stampede.

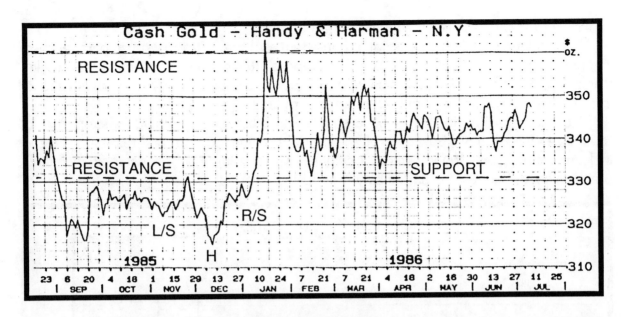

Cash Gold — Handy & Harman — N.Y.

RESISTANCE

RESISTANCE   SUPPORT

L/S   R/S

H   1985   1986

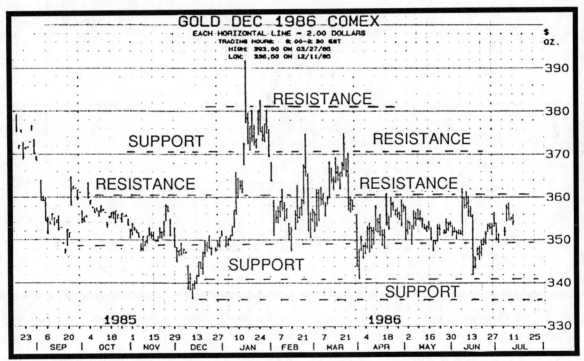

GOLD DEC 1986 COMEX
EACH HORIZONTAL LINE = 2.00 DOLLARS
TRADING HOURS: 8:00-2:30 EST
HIGH: 393.00 ON 03/27/86
LOW: 336.50 ON 12/11/85

RESISTANCE

SUPPORT   RESISTANCE

RESISTANCE   RESISTANCE

SUPPORT

SUPPORT

1985   1986

An oddity of gaps is the self-fulfilling saying of Futures markets, "Gaps get filled." Gaps tend to function like other support and resistance levels, drawing price back to trade where it missed trading because of the gap. This may happen in a matter of days, or it may take weeks, months or years.

After price is drawn to a gap, and ideally into it, the gap should act as a springboard for price to rebound and resume its travel in the direction of the gap. But if price goes through a gap and remains on the far side of it, the gap's role of support or resistance is reversed. It is the same as when price crosses a trendline or a channel line: price is then

77

expected to stay on the other side of the gap.

The incidence of filling gaps is not as consistent as the saying suggests, in part because it imposes no time parameters. However, it happens often enough that some traders make a point of placing orders in gaps when they appear, in the expectation that price will retrace into the gap, giving an opportunity to enter a trade at a good price.

The chart for March 1986 Cocoa shows numerous gaps working as support and resistance. It also shows how gaps often occur at previous support and resistance levels, including at old gaps. In fact, when price gaps over any support or resistance, including previous gaps, the event is particularly significant.

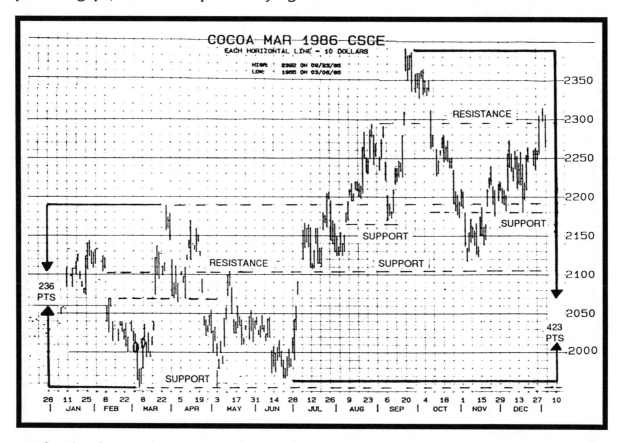

On the Cocoa chart, notice the significant level of support and resistance that was established at about the $2,100 level by the gap down in February 1985. Thereafter, this level drew price like a magnet. On July 8 price gapped powerfully up through it. The $2,100 level then provided rock-like support when tested four days later by a huge downside reversal.

It is useful to mark gaps (except for very obvious ones) on your charts with circles in colored ink. The Cocoa chart has gaps marked only during March and April to avoid obscuring the subsequent action.

Gaps on the *weekly* charts often have significance that can last for years. The five days of a normal business week comprise a complete unit of trading because many traders square their books for the weekend on Friday. Monday mornings usually see a surge in trading activity, as people act on their weekend homework and news affecting markets.

When this surge in activity also coincides with price gapping away on the opening, it can have more significance than a gap happening on any other day of the week. When a gap appears on the weekly chart, price must have gapped away on Monday morning and was unable to fill it during the rest of the week.

Look back at the weekly Gold chart (page 75) and see the lasting influence of the gap down in February 1983. Price retraced back into the gap two months later and stopped there. Then it came back to the same level three years later, in September 1986, where it again stopped and made a significant retracement.

GAPS FILLED ON A CLOSING BASIS

Although gaps suggest important and sudden new buying or selling pressure, it is seldom clear when the gap occurs whether this new pressure is temporary or longer lasting. We cannot know at the time whether an apparent breakaway or runaway gap will turn out to be an exhaustion gap.

If the new buying or selling pressure is truly dominant, price should continue in the direction that it has gapped. If, however, the gap is filled on a closing basis, we should assume that the forces of supply and demand have come back into equilibrium. In this case, a trade in the direction of the gap should generally be liquidated (as discussed in Chapter 13).

PRICE PROJECTIONS AND RETRACEMENTS: THE GOLDEN RULE

We have discussed why price moves from one level to another and then retraces part of the way back. A related and practical issue is how far price might travel once it breaks through support or resistance, and how far it might come back on a retracement.

One widely used method of calculating price projections is the so-called Golden Rule. It is based on the idea that price can be expected to advance and retrace by an amount proportional to certain ratios of previous advances and declines. These ratios are based on a concept attributed to Leonardo Fibonacci, also known as Leonardo of Pisa, who lived in the 13th Century. Fibonacci ratios are based on the ratio between any successive numbers of the Fibonacci sequence. This sequence starts with one and always adds the preceding number, as follows: 1,1, 2, 3, 5, 8, 13, 21, 34, 55, 89, etc. In turn, the sequence produces the ratios 1, 1/2, 2/3, 3/5, 5/8, etc.

The ratios after the first four numbers in the Fibonacci sequence round out, when reduced to decimals, to .618 and its reciprocal of 1.618. This proportion is often found in nature and was used by the ancient Greeks in architecture. It is also a standard proportion for playing cards and windows.

The proportions of the Golden Rule cannot be taken as gospel, as some practitioners of the Elliott Wave theory of technical forecasting seem to suggest. However, it provides the best available rule of thumb for trying to determine the potential extent of an advance or retracement before it happens.

The following proportions comprise the template for the percentages of possible retracement and advance:

Retracement	Advance
0.382 (1 - .618)	1.262
0.50 (2 - 1)	1.50
0.618	1.618

Standard theory states that a retracement approaching .618 of a previous move is regarded as normal and that doing so does not weaken the overall strength of a trend. Retracements in the vicinity of 60 to 65% occur extremely frequently, almost as if this ratio were imbued with royal jelly. An extension of the theory states that a retracement that much exceeds .618 of the previous move suggests the probability that the entire move will be given up and that the trend may possibly have changed.

Smaller retracements are likely to occur at .382 and .50 of a previous move. One approach to entering markets is to enter positions on a 50% retracement, with a stop-loss at 65%. While this approach is generally inferior to our concept of moving with the momentum of markets, it is useful to know what some other traders are looking at.

Applied to advances, Fibonacci ratios are used to project major advances in the proportion of 1.618 of the previous move, intermediate advances at 1.5 times the previous move and smaller advances at 1.262 times.

Fibonacci proportions should be used in conjunction with existing levels of support and resistance from previous market action. When a level of support or resistance coincides with one of the proportions from the Golden Rule's template, it is additionally probable that price will reach for that level and also turn there.

The Golden Rule is also useful when price is heading into uncharted territory where there is no previous experience of levels of support and resistance.

The long-term chart for cash Corn shows that in 1973 Corn moved out of the price range in which it had been confined for over 25 years, between $2.70 per bushel and 95¢, a range of $1.75. How far might this breakout go?

The Golden Rule calculations would be as follows:

1. Price range x   1.618   =   Potential amplitude of the advance
       $1.75   x   1.618   = $2.82

2. Potential amplitude +   Price at the breakout = Target price
       $2.82   + $1.10   = $3.82

If all this looks like magical retrofitting against the chart, you are right. However, there are circumstances such as this where it is useful to have parameters for guessing intelligently how far price might go. And you can also take comfort from knowing that a

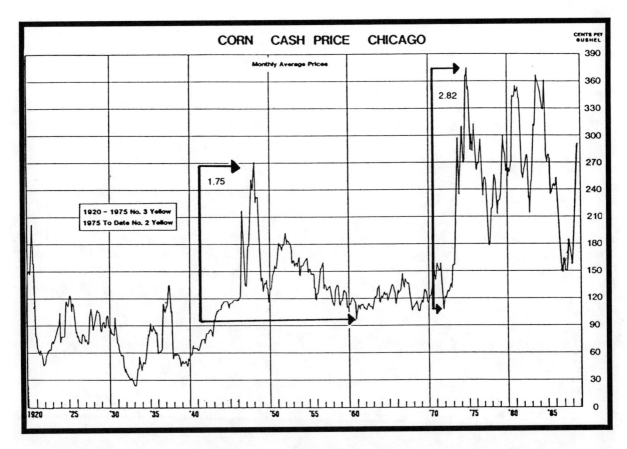

CORN   CASH PRICE   CHICAGO

lot of other people will be using the same formula and will be trading in accordance with its result.

The chart for March 1986 Cocoa (page 78) shows how the ratios of the Golden Rule work in the intermediate picture. During the spring, there was a major move up of 236 points. Without repeating the formula, the calculation for determining the price target for a further move up is: 236 x 1.618 = 382.

After the price cleared $2,190, you could project an expected top for the entire move at $2,337. Price happened to continue for a further 55 points. But it was a remarkable projection, considering that price gapped through the target price and made its top that day.

After the top, you could have used the Golden Rule to project how far the retracement might go. Using the extent of the move up, 433 points, the calculation is:

$$433 \times .618 = 268$$

The actual retracement was 253 points, stopping just above the major band of support at the $2,100 level.

Fibonacci ratios are so well known that they seem to be self-fulfilling. It is irrelevant whether their effect actually comes from internal or external forces. It is enough to know that many traders will buy and sell at prices related specifically to these numbers.

Chapter 12

Trading Ranges: What To Avoid And How To Profit From Them

In the previous two chapters, price action was compared with a sailboat tacking back and forth. But sometimes the wind subsides, the sails droop and the boat goes nowhere. The same thing happens when price becomes becalmed, going sideways for an indefinite time, until the wind — in the form of new buying or selling pressure — starts moving the market up or down again.

A sideways or trading range market can begin in any kind of market conditions when buying or selling pressure subsides. Price is confined within a relatively small range and usually between roughly horizontal support and resistance levels that will be apparent on both the daily and the weekly charts. Sometimes a trading range will form a triangular shape.

The size of a trading range would, for example, usually be a maximum of $20 to $30 in Gold or a few cents in Live Hogs. It would also, in general, be too restricted for development of a pattern of higher highs and higher lows (a bull market, as defined in Chapter 7) or a pattern of lower highs and lower lows (a bear market).

A trading range generally occurs when supply and demand are in equilibrium, which leads to a consensus about what constitutes a reasonable price. So there is little action in the market. Alternatively, a market may trade sideways while it is marking time, waiting for fresh fundamental news to give it direction. In either case, the trading range may last for a few weeks, months or even years. In addition, a trading range market often occurs in deferred agricultural contracts, particularly in Cattle and Live Hogs, although the nearby contracts will be in clearly trending markets.

It may be obvious but the point is worth stating: the prime opportunities for making money occur in markets that move up or down, ideally quickly and by a large amount, and not in markets that move sideways.

Furthermore, trading a sideways market can expose you to triple jeopardy. First, money tied up in trades waiting for something to happen is money that cannot be used when other potentially profitable opportunities arise. Second, there is a risk that the eventual breakout may be in the wrong direction. Third, you may have your trading equity eaten away if the carrying charges are working against you (discussed in Chapter 15).

Therefore, to make profits and avoid triple jeopardy:

1. Watch for the tell-tale signs of a becalmed market — and remind yourself to look for them.

2. Look for an opportunity to cover trades that are caught in a sideways market.

   Getting caught in a sideways market is sometimes unavoidable, since a trading range, by definition, must exist for at least a few weeks before it becomes clear that it is one. Eventually there should be a signal to liquidate a trade because of price crossing a trendline, but you may be able to get out at a better price at your leisure.

3. Don't enter positions in a trading range market until it shows that it is preparing to break out (discussed below).

4. Despite these warnings to avoid having positions in a trading range market, watch for trading ranges, particularly long-lasting ones, because of the opportunities that occur when price breaks out of them.

   The longer a trading range lasts, the greater will be the complacency about the existing price equilibrium. Consequently, some of the most powerful trades occur when this equilibrium is disturbed.

   The guidelines for entering such trades follow.

HOW TO BUY AN EXPECTED BREAKOUT

Particularly when price has been in a trading range at a relatively low price level, use trading formations and entry rules to buy when:

a) price is positioned for a surge through the horizontal resistance line as well as any downtrend line in existence on the *weekly* chart; and

b) a W-Formation is being completed on the weekly chart, ideally with a low that forms well above the bottom of the trading range.

The weekly chart for Copper shows only five opportunities to buy on potential breakouts from a trading range that lasted for three years.
The first opportunity to buy, in early 1985, fulfilled the above parameters for buying.

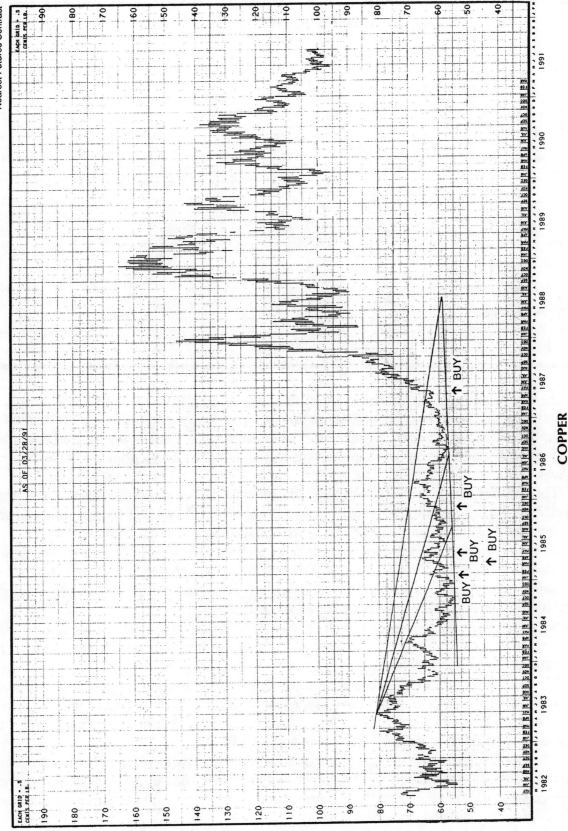

Commodity Exchange, Inc.
Weekly High, Low, Friday Close
Nearest Futures Contract

EACH GRID = .5
CENTS PER LB.

AS OF 03/28/91

EACH GRID = .5
CENTS PER LB.

COPPER

85

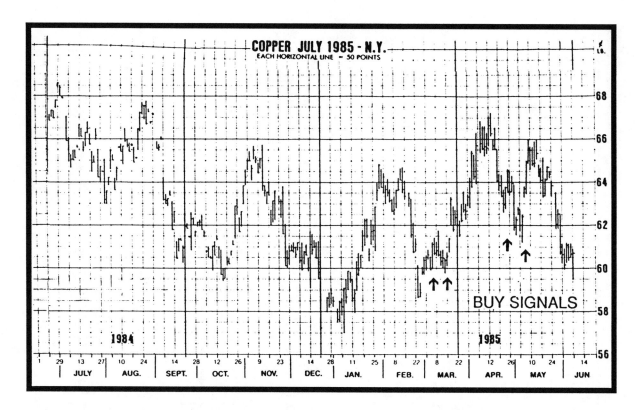

COPPER JULY 1985 - N.Y.
EACH HORIZONTAL LINE = 50 POINTS

BUY SIGNALS

1984

1985

| | JULY | AUG. | SEPT. | OCT. | NOV. | DEC. | JAN. | FEB. | MAR. | APR. | MAY | JUN |

There was a textbook W-Formation and its completion coincided with price gapping simultaneously over the major resistance line and the downtrend line. The trade didn't work, but it was a valid entry signal. After price retraced below the downtrend line, the case for entering trades on the long side was negated until a good higher low for a second W was completed.

The second major entry to the long side of the Copper market occurred after the retracement from this initial breakout. The daily chart for July 1985 Copper shows two possible entries on the basis of trading formations, on March 6 and 15.

Although the high in February on this chart was below the level of the November high, this does not negate the trade. The chart shows the impact of carrying charges and does not reflect the forces of supply and demand working on the cash price. This is one reason why we use weekly charts for defining major trends.

After entering the market in March, we would keep on working the long side of the market, trading out on signals to liquidate (or on being stopped out) and re-entering on delivery of the next signal to buy.

The buy signal in March worked well; depending on your precise entry, you would have banked about four or five cents after getting out on a signal to liquidate. This trade was followed by a buy signal on April 25 that didn't work. Finally, there was a third entry in May which would have delivered a further good profit.

After that, there wasn't another trade until December. The lower high in May signaled the failure of the bull market, the emergence of an erratic market and a new downtrend line on the weekly chart. All of these combined to indicate a stand-aside market until the sideways action showed signs of changing.

86

HOW TO SELL AN EXPECTED BREAKOUT

The procedure for selling an expected breakout is the same as for buying, only in reverse.

Use trading formations and entry rules to sell when:

a) price is positioned for a surge through the horizontal support line as well as any uptrend line in existence on the *weekly* chart; and

b) an M-Formation is being completed on the weekly chart, ideally with a high that forms well below the top of the trading range.

TRIANGLES

Triangles differ from trading ranges in that the lines of support and resistance converge. This means that within a triangle, unlike a trading range bounded by horizontal lines, price is confined by time. It has to break out in one direction or the other before it reaches the apex. The assumption is that a worthwhile surge will occur when the face-off between buyers and sellers ends on the breakout. Triangles comprise a form of coiling action from which a major surge is likely to follow when the compression is released.

When looking at triangles to see which way the break is likely to occur, pay particular attention to daily price action as an indicator of buying or selling pressure. The Wellspring System's concept of noting where price closes in relation to the daily range is very valuable for suggesting when and in which direction price may break out of any congestion area.

1. Ascending and Descending Triangles

The chart for March 1986 Corn on page 88 shows both an ascending triangle and a descending triangle.

For an ascending triangle, draw an upward sloping line (usually an uptrend line) to join rising lows, which show accumulation. Across the top of the highs, where price has topped two or more times at the same level, draw a horizontal line. The expectation is that price will ultimately move up through the horizontal line, usually with a significant surge in price.

Descending triangles are the opposite of ascending triangles, having a horizontal line drawn across lows and a downward sloping line to join declining highs, which show distribution. Hence, the expectation is that price will break out on the downside.

Notice how both of the breakouts from the triangles shown on the Corn chart were followed by price retracing to the horizontal lines that had previously provided support and resistance respectively.

2. Symmetrical Triangles

Symmetrical triangles consist of a trading range in which both highs and lows contract

CORN MAR 1986 CBOT

EACH HORIZONTAL LINE = 2 CENTS

HIGH 297 ON 11/12/84
LOW 224-4 ON 09/06/85

DESCENDING TRIANGLE

ASCENDING TRIANGLE

and the apex of the resulting triangle is approximately in the middle of the price range.

The expectation is that there will be a significant move one way or the other when the face-off between buyers and sellers is resolved, and that price will continue in the direction of the breakout. The triangle does not, of itself, suggest in which direction the breakout will come. However, our trading formation and entry rules should normally get you into trades in the direction of the move and keep you out of markets making a false breakout, where price turns back in the opposite direction.

The chart for December 1985 T-Bonds shows how the breakout to the upside from a symmetrical triangle coincided with an upside weekly reversal, a Lindahl buy signal and five consecutively higher closes. Despite all these powerful indicators, price still had to retrace to the breakout side of the triangle, as also occurred on the Corn chart.

3. Triangles on the Weekly Charts

As with many of our indicators, triangles can also serve as an important indicator when applied to weekly charts.

A roughly symmetrical triangle formed on the weekly Copper chart during 1983. When price gapped through the uptrend line, it signaled the beginning of a very substantial and rapid decline.

88

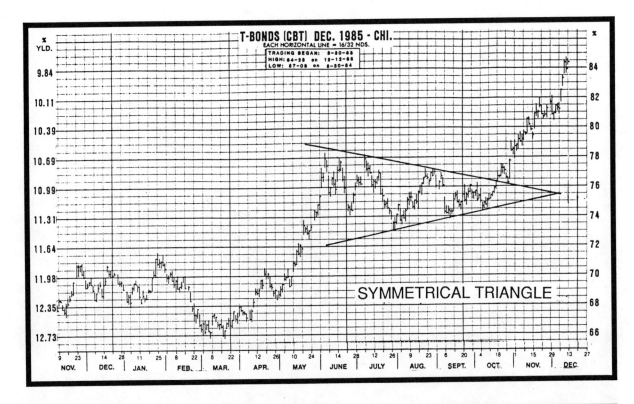

SYMMETRICAL TRIANGLE

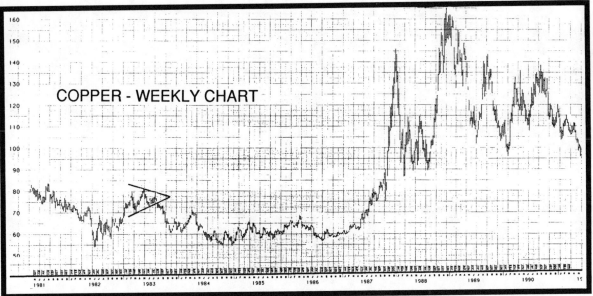

COPPER - WEEKLY CHART

89

Chapter 13

Stops And Liquidation Of Trades

The procedures for stops and liquidation of trades are described in the form of rules so as to make them easy to learn.

Since it's easier to follow rules when you know the philosophy behind them, let's first consider the following principles.

1. The purpose of stops is to protect trading capital and unrealized profits.

   When a market stops performing in accordance with your expectations, including predetermined tolerances, you should close out the trade. Staying with a trade that goes off track by exceeding your guidelines for trading is like maintaining full speed ahead when you've driven your car off the road. The probability is high that you'll end up in the willows!

2. Getting stopped out of a trade is part of the way that Futures work. There will always be times when a trade is stopped out at a loss, or with only a small profit, although staying with the trade would have delivered large profits.

3. Markets are always right: they don't know or care where you got into a trade or why. Therefore, in deciding whether to stay in a trade, the only valid consideration is what to do in relation to current market action, not whether you have a profit or a loss.

   This area of Futures decision-making probably contains the most difficult psychological hurdles for traders. Everyone wants to book profits. But Murphy's Law of Futures Trading means that profitable trades will make more profit after you get out, and losing trades will make bigger losses if you don't.

4. If you are unwilling to use stops at all times, under all circumstances, you should not be trading Futures.

You cannot trade without the discipline of stops, even if they are a long way from your entry price, any more than you can responsibly drive a car without insurance. At the very least, stops serve the dual purpose of saving you from the misery of your own indecision and from unexpected disaster.

One of the reasons why people don't use stops is that they don't have a reliable means of entering profitable trades; so they don't trust their procedure either for placing stops or liquidating positions. You are entitled to *believe* that the Wellspring System works. Therefore, you *must* follow its rules for taking both profits and losses, and accept the fact that perfection in placing stops and liquidating trades is simply not an achievable part of the business.

5. When considering a new entry after a trade has been stopped out or liquidated, it is *not* significant whether you enter at a better or worse price than where you got out.

   You must look at every new trade on its own merits. Don't ever consider how much was made or lost on the last trade or whether re-entering means foregoing some potential profit that would have been kept had you not got out of the market.

6. Stops are not a substitute for closing out trades in accordance with the rules for *liquidating* trades.

   Some people use stops as the only means of liquidating trades. This procedure transfers the psychological burden of making a decision to liquidate from the trader to the market. This approach will make money with good entry techniques but it will not maximize profits.

7. The best defense against the grief of having positions stopped out at a loss is to be patient in stalking the best trades and to take the strongest signals.

   Remember that there is no shortage of trading opportunities having several positive confirming indicators, so there is no need to take second rate signals.

RULES FOR ENTERING STOPS

These rules are illustrated on the September 1989 Eurodollar chart on page 95.

Stop Rule 1

Use Stop Close Only (SCO) orders rather than open stops, except:

a) for Stock Index Futures and other contracts having the capability for immense intra-day moves (which will depend on market conditions);

b) for positions showing a substantial profit where a turn in the market could be expected; and

c) after a limit move in the direction of your trade. (Retracements can be violent when the limit move is an expression of exhaustion.)

Ordinary stops and SCO orders both preserve trading capital and avert disastrous losses. SCO orders, activated in the last five minutes of the trading day, will result in fewer profitable trades being stopped out prematurely. The problem with ordinary open stops is that floor traders will often deliberately push the market during the day to run the stops and clean them out for their own profit. When stopped out with SCO orders, losses will tend to be larger and profits smaller than with ordinary stops. But you should make more money, on balance, because the proportion of profitable trades should increase.

SCO orders are not accepted by all exchanges. However, your broker should be able to handle them for you where the exchange doesn't take them. If the broker doesn't agree to do so, find one who will.

Stop Rule 2

Place *open orders* that are Good Till Canceled (GTC).

While you can place stop orders that are good only for the day, they do not do the job of providing the insurance that you need all the time. Consider, as a worst case, what could happen to your account (or to your estate) if you were run over by a bus before placing stops the next morning.

Stop Rule 3

Immediately after entering a position (or simultaneously), enter an Initial Protective Stop (IPS):

a) just beyond the trading formation giving the signal to enter the market; or

b) when there is a *breakaway or runaway gap*, at a level where the gap would be filled on a closing basis. (This is therefore entered as an SCO order.)

There will usually be an identifiable spike on the chart at the beginning of a trading formation; the stop is placed just beyond the spike. Although one tick above the high or below the low does the job, it is preferable to place a stop one or two ticks beyond a round number if one is close to the stop point. Thus a protective sell-stop for Eurodollars might be placed at 89.95 if the low of the entry formation was at 90.02.

Rule 3(b) does essentially the same job as Exit Rule 2, described on page 99. It is included in order to handle situations where you are unable to assess the day's action as the market is going into the close.

Stop Rule 4

Move the protective stop to a point just beyond each new spike or trading formation when it is completed.

The IPS and subsequent protective stops marked on the September 1989 Eurodollar chart show how stops are moved progressively when the trade works in the expected direction. In real trading, though, we would have been in and out of the market a few times, as described in the rules for liquidating trades, in order to avert the risk of giving back too much profit.

Stop Rule 5

Enter stops closer than identifiable spikes or chart points *only* when there is an identifiable risk of a substantial reversal when one or more of the following conditions exists:

a) price is approaching a major support or resistance level, a channel line or a major trendline;

b) a cycle low (when short) is expected after a sustained decline or a cycle high (when long) is expected after a sustained advance (discussed in Chapter 17); and/or

c) the RSI and stochastics are very oversold (when short) or (when long) very overbought (discussed in Chapter 19).

Under these circumstances, use ordinary stops (not SCO orders) and give the market just a little room to move; for instance, to a point just beyond the previous day's high when short, or the previous day's low when long, or about half a limit move. Sometimes a short-term trendline (discussed in Chapter 10) may help in deciding where to place the stop.

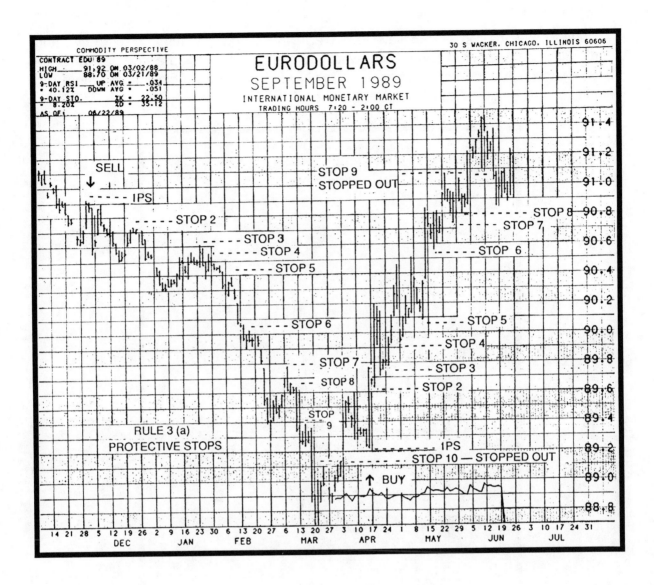

Stop Rule 6

Do not change the place for the IPS or subsequent protective stops when there are very powerful signals.

It is an irony of trading Futures that trades with powerful signals, and thus the potential for large and immediate profits, often require stops that would result in a large drawdown if hit.

The remedy is not to avoid these trades, because passing them up means missing some of the best opportunities. Neither is the remedy to sneak stops in closer than the rules require. Risk is usually in inverse proportion to the power of the signal. Nevertheless, moving stops closer invites an unnecessary loss: even markets with the most powerful entry signals, including gaps, may retrace without weakening the potential for the trade.

The remedy, instead, is to believe in powerful entry signals when you see them, and to adjust the number of contracts to what you can afford should the stop be hit. Once you have taken a few of these trades, you will feel more comfortable entering them and placing stops that seem quite distant.

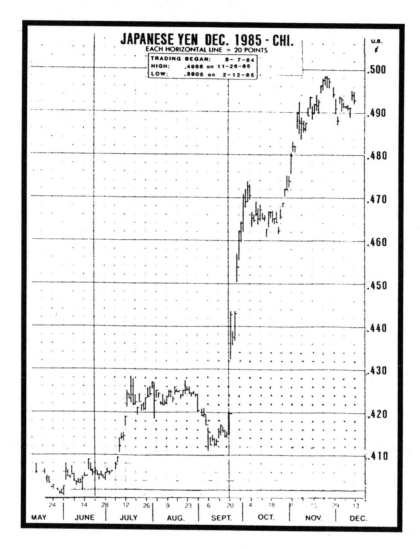

The chart for the December 1985 Japanese Yen shows a good example of this kind of situation. The weekly chart had already indicated that the Yen was in a new uptrend. The daily chart showed conventional buy signals at .4165 (the three-day rule) and at .4200 (the regular reversal rule). While the reversal suggested a trade with good average potential, the probability of a very powerful move was indicated only the next day with a gap up to .4435.

Entry with the major breakout required recognizing that price could retrace to the bottom of the gap or reversal day without diminishing the potential for the trade. Thus, the stop would be below the entry formation that delivered a buy signal or below .4140. Entering a trade at .4435 and having the stop hit at .4135 would result in a loss of $3,750. In fact, however, a trade entered at .4435 experienced only a tiny retracement initially before going on to deliver a profit of $6,450 when liquidated in January (not shown on the chart; assumes a rollover).

In sum, the challenge of taking the most powerful signals as a means of making the most money with the lowest overall exposure to risk is not a function of the entry signals as such, or of the stops. It is a function of psychological preparedness and capital management.

Stop Rule 7

When a trade is entered in accordance with Entry Rule 3, Early Entry (described in Chapter 5), enter an ordinary day stop on the following basis:

a) after the market has been open for an hour, either just under the low for the day up to that time when buying, or just above the high when selling; or

b) just under the previous day's low when buying, or the previous day's high when selling.

The early entry rule overrides the Wellspring System's normal approach of making decisions on the basis of closing prices. Early entry is likely to lead either to spectacular success or spectacular failure when you are trading in the direction of a gap. But the failures can be contained by the use of ordinary day stops.

Generally, we don't like taking a short-term view. So it is important not to let action based on trying to get an advantage from one day's trading turn into a nightmare. When a trade entered early doesn't lead to an immediate profit, you are probably better off to act on the adage, "Never take a loss home overnight!" Unless you believe there is a compelling reason to stay in, get out of the trade. If you stay in, enter a regular open stop.

RULES FOR LIQUIDATING TRADES (EXIT RULES)

While the use of stops is mandatory as insurance, the majority of trades will be liquidated in accordance with parameters dictating an exit from the market prior to getting stopped out. Waiting for stops to be hit means giving back too much profit or incurring an unnecessarily large loss. Exiting as soon as a trade starts to misbehave prevents a correction from getting out of hand and preserves profits.

It is both impractical and psychologically difficult to wrestle with the decision as to whether to stay in a trade when a correction starts to look like a new trend in the opposite direction. It's much better to get out when trades start to correct against you. You can always get back in again when the next entry signal is delivered.

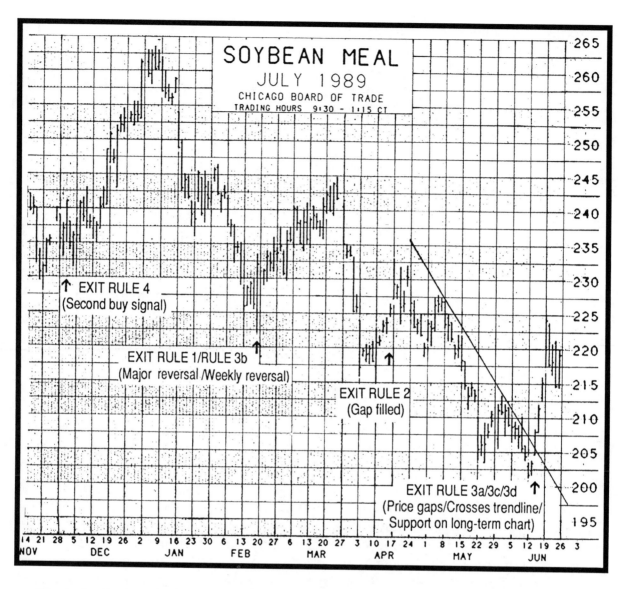

The rules for liquidating trades are illustrated on the chart for July 1989 Soybean Meal above. References to buy signals in a bear market mean only that you cover short positions, not that you go long — and vice versa for a bull market.

Exit Rule 1

Liquidate trades immediately when a single *major* reversal day against the trend occurs.

A reversal day is major when it has:

a) a range twice as large as that of the previous day and/or recent days; and

b) a close in the top 25% of the day's range when you are short, or in the bottom 25% of the day's range when you are long.

Coincident indicators will often also suggest the possibility of at least a short-term correction against the established trend.

Exit Rule 2

Liquidate trades when a breakaway gap or a runaway gap is filled on a closing basis *and* price closes at the extreme end of the range *against* the trade.

Exit Rule 3

Liquidate trades immediately when a signal to trade in the opposite direction (described in Chapters 4 and 5 on trading formations and entry rules) is completed and when one or more of the following also occurs:

a) price gaps against the trade (except when the gap is small and price remains confined within a consolidation);

b) a weekly reversal has been completed recently or simultaneously (Friday is the important day from a weekly standpoint, although some chart services use the heavy line to designate Mondays);

c) price crosses a short-term trendline (also described in Chapter 10, Trendline Principle 5(b)); and/or

d) the trade has reached an important level of support or resistance, such as a previous significant high or low, or a channel line.

Exit Rule 4

Liquidate trades immediately when a *second* consecutive signal to enter a trade in the opposite direction is completed.

One signal to trade in the opposite direction may just be an aberration; a second signal is likely to be the start of something more serious.

Exit Rule 5

Liquidate trades immediately when a limit move against the trade appears imminent or, for those contracts not having limits, when any sudden and very large move against the trade comes out of the blue.

Limits exist only for certain Futures contracts. Limit moves occur often in some Futures, such as Pork Bellies, but seldom in others. The point of this rule is that you don't want to be exposed to further unquantifiable adverse movement in price over which you have no control.

Rather than place a stop order every day just inside a limit move, have your broker use his best efforts to see that you never get caught in a limit move against you.

Exit Rule 6

Do not liquidate trades without a clear signal to do so.

There is almost always a trade-off when trying to distinguish between a minor aberration and a potentially more significant correction. The Eurodollar chart (page 95) shows a very persistent market, both up and down, where it would have been easy just to sit through minor fluctuations. On the other hand, the Soybean Meal chart (page 98) shows how even routine retracements can give back a lot of profit and can last for several weeks.

DON'T BE IMPATIENT

Some traders enter markets after price has retraced for three days against an established trend. You can see from the Soybean Meal chart why this is an unsatisfactory concept, but it is worth knowing that some traders regard retracements as an opportunity to enter trades rather than to liquidate them. The Wellspring System identifies retracements early while not reacting to every hiccup.

The greatest stress in handling trades occurs before they start to make money. This is when some traders are most tempted to liquidate their positions prematurely. When in doubt, you are usually better off to let the initial protective stop do the work of getting you out of a trade that doesn't get under way immediately. Particularly after entering a market in response to the three-day rule or the Lindahl rule, buyers and sellers may have to finish their face-off before the trade can move ahead.

It is also tempting to throw the towel in prematurely when price is merely testing support or resistance in a gap. A gap that is merely tested, without being filled on a closing basis, is likely to act as a spring that propels price in the desired direction.

Where there is a succession of gaps, as sometimes occurs in very fast moving markets, price may have to fill earlier gaps before resuming its major direction. This is illustrated on the chart for August 1986 Crude Oil.

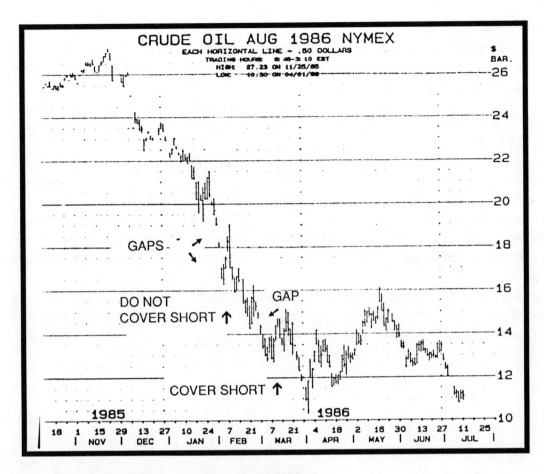

CRUDE OIL AUG 1986 NYMEX
EACH HORIZONTAL LINE ~ .50 DOLLARS
TRADING HOURS 9:45-3:10 EST
HIGH 27.23 ON 11/25/85
LOW 10.50 ON 04/01/86

GAPS

DO NOT
COVER SHORT ↑

GAP

COVER SHORT ↑

1985   1986

TAKING PROFITS AT ROUND NUMBERS

Prices will tend to aim for big round numbers as a target *and go through them* before reversing and setting in motion a major correction, if not a change of trend. Therefore, don't be fooled by a close above or below a big round number, since there is a high probability of it being a sucker play.

Examples abound of price heading for round numbers and being turned back. Among the most prominent are the turns made by the Dow Jones Industrial Average at the 1,000 level and at the 3,000 level.

Sometimes these round numbers may exist as reciprocals in currency markets or as round numbers relating to yield, rather than price, in interest rate Futures.

When a trade approaches an important round number, be prepared to close it out right away or enter a close stop, rather than wait to be caught by a sudden and violent retracement.

STOPS — HOUSEKEEPING

Open orders remain in force for the life of the contract or until you cancel them. Stops are not canceled automatically when positions are liquidated. Only day stops expire at the end of the trading day.

The responsibility for canceling open stops rests with you, not the broker. Open orders left outstanding can lead to unpleasant surprises, including fills and delivery notices just before expiration of a contract.

You must, therefore, keep an accurate record of open orders in your order book. It is useful to mark them with a highlighter felt pen in order to draw attention to them when closing out a position.

You should also go over your open orders with the broker to make sure that you agree with what's outstanding. Brokers would far prefer to spend a few moments checking open orders than have to sort out a mess with a trade entered by mistake.

When taking a profit, it is a good idea from a psychological point of view to check whether you should not also get out of any losing positions. Too many people close out their profitable positions and keep their losers — the opposite of what is required to make money!

Set regular times for reviewing positions and liquidating bad ones. Thursday night is a good time, for action on Friday morning, before the potential volatility arising from everyone else squaring books for the weekend.

Chapter 14

Putting The Signals To Work

We have now completed the basic study of the Wellspring System's rules and principles for entering markets, and for stops and the liquidation of trades. Although there are additional indicators, described in the following chapters, to help select markets to trade, this is a good point to stop and work through an exercise in simulated trading.

Remember that it is an important component of the system that we don't wait around in trades where the market starts to misbehave. On the other hand, we try not to twitch prematurely by liquidating trades simply because they don't feel good. Therefore, we follow the rules for entering trades, as well as the rules for stops and for getting out, with as much attention to detail as possible. An important corollary of getting out relatively fast in order to protect profits and to avert losses is that we re-enter immediately on delivery of the next signal, provided that the overall picture relating to the trend is favorable.

Think of finding a good market to work as you would think of finding a good fishing lake. You may not get a good catch every time you go out, but if you keep on working the lake systematically and patiently, the chances are that you will have a steady supply of fish for supper as well as some for the freezer.

You will notice that even in the most favorable markets there is an average of only about one good trade per month. That is normal. You do *not* have to be in the market all the time. If you average more than about one completed trade per month in any market, you are probably trading too much. Of course, the average over a longer period will consist of some trades lasting only a day or two, usually the losers, and some that may last for well over a month.

The September 1989 Standard & Poor Stock Index Futures chart is used to illustrate how to apply the signals to trade. You can see from the weekly chart superimposed on the daily chart that the S&P was in a strong bull market, with a succession of higher highs and higher lows. Therefore, as required by Chapter 7, trades would be taken only on the long side. The first entry is marked (1) on the weekly chart and the last exit is marked (5).

It is worth noting that the S&P began to accelerate after closing the gap on the weekly

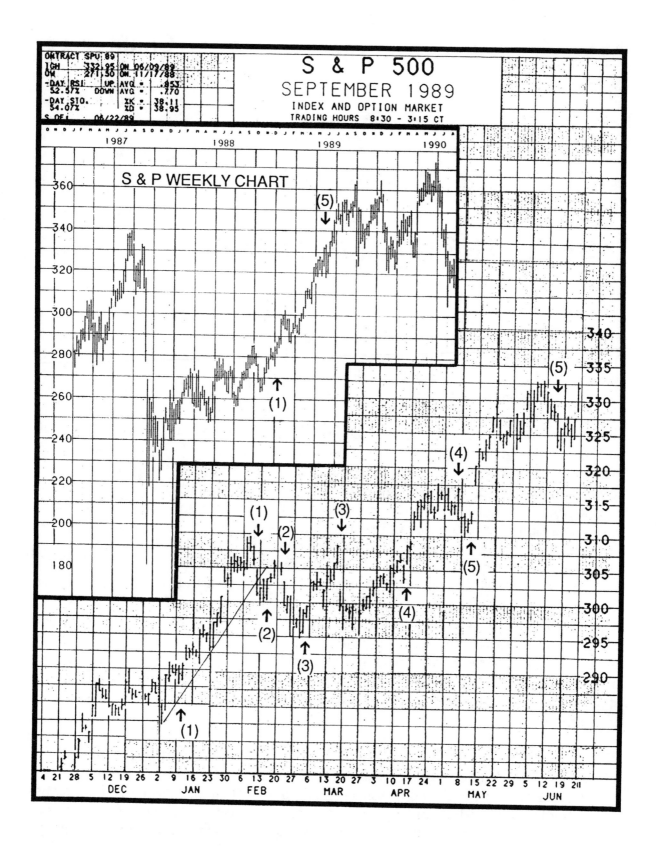

S & P 500
SEPTEMBER 1989
INDEX AND OPTION MARKET
TRADING HOURS 8:30 - 3:15 CT

S & P WEEKLY CHART

chart left behind from the 1987 crash. Until the gap was closed, there was a reasonable probability that the advance would be contained at that level.

The daily chart for this S&P contract does not show any individual days of huge volatility. However, the weekly chart for the period following exit (5) shows how suddenly it can appear. That is why Stop Rule 1 recommends that ordinary open stops, rather than SCO orders, be used for the S&P, as well as any other markets liable to be struck suddenly by a hurricane.

The S&P chart shows price moving with a lot of gaps. In practice, you would have to be sure to liquidate any trade where the gap was filled on a closing basis, in accordance with Exit Rule 2, rather than wait for the open stop to be hit. (You could enter two stops on an OCO basis — one order cancels the other — but this is complicated.)

Five trades were taken during the period covered by the September 1989 S&P chart. The dates refer to that day's trading action. The date for moving a stop, for example, refers to the close that dictates the action, even though the order might arrive at the exchange the next morning, before the opening.

Take time to work through these sample trades. Then find some charts at random and work through the rules of the Wellspring System yourself so that you become thoroughly familiar with it, as well as confident in your ability to use it.

Trade #1

Date	Entry/Exit	Stops	Basis For Action	Profit/Loss
Jan. 11	Buy @ 290.50		Ch. 8 - Weekly upside reversal the previous week	
			Ch. 4 - Rule 1 (3-Day), Rule 5 (Lindahl) Ch. 5 - Rule 1(a) Buy	
		IPS 287.50	Ch. 13 - Stop Rules 1, 2, 3(a)	
Jan. 18		Move to 290.50	Ch. 13 - Stop Rule 4	
Jan. 24		Move to 292.50	Ch. 13 - Stop Rule 4	
Jan. 31		Move to 300.50	Ch. 13 - Stop Rule 4	
Feb. 7		Move to 303.50	Ch. 13 - Stop Rule 4	
Feb. 10	Sell @ 303.50		Stopped out	$6,500

Comments on Trade #1

1. In view of the powerful weekly key reversal the previous week and the potential for completing a Lindahl formation, it would have been acceptable to enter a long position during the day of January 11 (Chapter 5, Entry Rule 3, Early Entry).

Trade #2

Date	Entry/Exit	Stops	Basis For Action	Profit/Loss
Feb. 15	Buy @ 303.50		Ch. 4 - Rule 8 (Double Reversal)	
			Ch. 5 - Rule 1(a) Buy	
		IPS 299.50	Ch. 13 - Stop Rules 1, 2, 3(a)	
Feb. 22	Sell @ 299.50		Stopped out	($2,000)

Comments on Trade #2

1. Although there were some negative factors working against this trade, an entry has been assumed so that you can see why some trades may not work out. The negative factors are:
   a) a very powerful downside weekly reversal the previous week (Chapter 7);
   b) price had crossed over the short-term downtrend line (Chapter 10);
   c) the gap down suggested that there might be significant resistance at the 305.00 level (Chapter 11).

2. This trade shows the importance of entering as soon as the signal is delivered, if you're going to take it at all. The size of the loss, at $2,000, was very manageable in the overall scheme of trading the S&P. An entry delayed until February 17, the next day, when price closed in the top 25% of the range (Chapter 5, Rule 1(a) Buy), would have led to an increase in the loss by $1,000.

Trade #3

Date	Entry/Exit	Stops	Basis For Action	Profit/Loss
March 3	Buy @ 299.50		Ch. 4 - Rule 2 (Regular Reversal)	
			Ch. 5 - Rule 1(a) Buy	
		IPS 294.50	Ch. 13 - Stop Rules 1, 2, 3(a)	
March 13		Move to 299.40	Ch. 13 - Stop Rule 4	
March 6		Move to 302.50	Ch. 13 - Stop Rule 4	
March 17	Sell @ 301.80		Stopped out	$1,150

Comments on Trade #3

1. As with Trade #2, this trade demonstrates the importance of taking entry signals as soon as they are delivered. Timely entry permitted banking a small profit, whereas entry delayed until the next day would have resulted in a $2,000 loss.

Trade #4

Date	Entry/Exit	Stops	Basis For Action	Profit/Loss
April 14	Buy @ 308.50		Ch. 4 - Rule 6 (Trend Continuation)	
			Ch. 4 - Rule 4 (Island)	
		IPS 302.50	Ch. 13 - Stop Rules 1, 2, 3(a)	
May 5	Sell @ 312.50		Ch. 7 - Downside weekly reversal the previous week	$2,000
			Ch. 13 - Exit Rule 1 (major reversal)	

Comments on Trade #4

1. You might have entered on April 7, given the substantial key reversal day accompanying completion of a trading formation (Rule 1, three-day rule and Rule 2, regular reversal rule). However, the huge gap down on March 17 should have made you realize that the market was vulnerable to stalling out again as it approached resistance at about 306.00. The overall picture could be regarded as an emerging W-Formation having an initial higher low, which would qualify for an entry on a breakout above 306.00. Until the breakout, the market looked as if it could go into a trading range.

2. The entry on April 14 could be taken as being, for all practical purposes, a breakout, although it didn't clearly pass the previous high. However, the power of the reversal was substantial. Technically, the qualification of Rule 4, the island rule, might be pushing its interpretation slightly but it is included to illustrate the concept of this rule.

3. The trade might have been liquidated three days earlier, on May 2. However, the overall picture was still looking very powerful and the gap underneath suggested that the consolidation might end soon. However, the powerful downside key reversal on May 5 could not be ignored, particularly after the weekly downside reversal the week before.

Trade #5

Date	Entry/Exit	Stops	Basis For Action	Profit/Loss
May 11	Buy @ 313.50		Ch. 4 - Rule 1 (3-Day) Ch. 5 - Rule 1(a) Buy	
		IPS 309.50	Ch. 13 - Stop Rules 1, 2, 3(a)	
May 12		Move to 311.50	Ch. 13 - Stop Rule 4	
May 15		Move to 317.00	Ch. 13 - Stop Rule 4	
May 17		Move to 320.50	Ch. 13 - Stop Rule 4	
May 24		Move to 322.50	Ch. 13 - Stop Rule 4	
June 6		Move to 326.00	Ch. 13 - Stop Rule 4	
June 15	Sell @ 326.00		Stopped out	$6,250

Comments on Trade #5

1. There were four days of price closing in the upper half of the day's range when the trading formation (Rule 1, three-day rule) was completed on May 11. On day 3, price failed to close in the top 25% of the range so entry was delayed for an additional day. However, the additional day of waiting also reinforced the validity of the support that the market was clearly finding in the gap.

2. If you missed the trade on May 11, it could have been taken on the gap up early on May 12, or on the close. This was a very powerful day, showing how power can feed on itself once a market gets up a good head of steam. May 12 is a good example of a day for using the early entry rule (Chapter 5, Entry Rule 3).

3. The reversal day and closing of the small gap on May 23 might have led you to liquidate, and it would have been acceptable to do so. However, we don't like to twitch too quickly when a market is going powerfully our way, preferring to delay a day or two as we also did at the end of trade #4. Had you gotten out, you would, in any case, have re-entered two days later, at a price about 100 points above your exit point.

SUMMARY

Over a period of five months, there were five completed trades. Profits totaled $13,900, trading one contract with no pyramiding, and the single loss was $2,000 (both excluding commissions and slippage).

This example demonstrates the merits of the Wellspring System's approach of patiently waiting for the trades with the greatest potential, always using stops and liquidating trades as soon as they misbehave.

Chapter 15

Normal And Inverted Markets

The previous chapter provided a pause to put into practice the core rules and principles of the Wellspring System. Chapters 15 to 20 describe several additional indicators that are essential for fine-tuning your trading. Chapters 21 to 24 discuss non-technical but important aspects of trading. Chapter 25 tells you how to put it all together.

This chapter alone provides insights that could make major additions to your trading profits, as well as help to steer you away from losses.

NORMAL MARKETS

You will see from a list of Futures price quotations that contracts for different delivery months have different prices, with the deferred months generally more expensive. Cash commodity prices, which are listed separately in newspapers and shown in some chart services, will generally be close to the price of nearest Futures, since Futures become cash at expiration.

Occasionally, imbalances in supply and demand lead to aberrations in the normal relationship between different delivery months. This chapter shows how normal relationships between delivery months can work either for or against you, and how aberrations from normality can indicate markets offering superior opportunity for profitable trades.

In a normal carrying charge market for physical commodities, the price of deferred Futures is progressively higher the more distant the expiration. Normality reflects the cash price of the commodity plus the cost of storage, insurance and interest on the money to pay for it (carrying charge).

Normality in Interest Rate Futures is the opposite. Deferred contracts usually stand at progressively greater discounts because owners of the actual bonds or bills receive interest in the meantime.

In agricultural commodities, seasonal factors are superimposed on markets. Prices tend to be lowest at harvest time when growers can deliver right off the land for cash, instead of having to store and double-handle the crop. Supply and demand expectations in relation to current stocks (old crop) and stocks not yet harvested, or perhaps not even planted (new crop), also affect price relationships.

Meat prices tend to be highest in spring or summer when North American demand is highest, but there is no standard relationship between prices for different delivery months.

Under normal circumstances, most nearby Futures contracts will fluctuate more — in both directions — than the deferred contracts. Thus a spread-trader expecting Cattle to go higher might buy the February contract and sell the June. If he were expecting prices overall to decline, he would sell the February and buy the June. (The Wellspring System does not recommend spreads as a vehicle for trading, primarily because spreads lock you into having a perspective on time and price that is inflexible. Another problem is that spreads can offer two opportunities to lose money, not make money, if both sides of the trade go in the wrong direction. However, there can be specialized applications for spreading that involve hedging and tax straddles.)

The greater fluctuation expected in nearby Futures dictates that we trade in nearer contracts rather than the deferred, unless there is a very good reason for going further out. The apparently lower risk involved in trading contracts that fluctuate less actually reduces profits more than it reduces risk.

The exception to the desirability of trading nearby contracts occurs when there is a conspicuous difference in the strength or weakness of deferred contracts compared with the nearby. If such a conspicuous difference exists, buy the stronger or sell the weaker. When entering a trade at the crest of an assumed emerging bear market, though, stay with the nearby contract because it will fall further.

CARRYING CHARGES CAN AFFECT PROFITS AND LOSSES

Assume for the purpose of illustration that cash Copper is trading at 60¢ and that Copper for one year delivery (one year deferred Futures) is trading at 66¢. If the cash price remains constant, the one year Futures will decline to 60¢ at expiration. This would result in a loss of 6¢ or $1,500 for each contract held long for the year. On the other hand, a holder of a short position under the same circumstances would make a profit of 6¢ or $1,500 per contract.

When taking a position where the carrying charges are working against you, as they are in the long Copper example, you must have reasonable price movement or the carrying charges will slowly eat up your equity. If the margin for a Copper contract is about $1,500, you can see that there is the potential to make a return of roughly plus or minus 100% annually on your money, depending on which side of the market you trade, if the cash price remains constant.

The carrying charge works the opposite way for long positions in U.S. Treasury Bonds. Here the buyer normally receives the equivalent of the carrying charge (in the form of interest that an owner of actual bonds would receive), while a short-seller would be adversely affected by Futures rising toward cash.

In the past few years there have been several markets, including Petroleum and the Canadian Dollar, where many traders have been badly hurt by a lack of awareness of which side of the carrying charges they were trading. Throughout the 1980s, Petroleum, for example, was expected by many to decline substantially. Therefore, the price of deferred Futures generally traded at progressively greater discounts, as traders pressed the short side of the market and consumers declined to make heavy forward commitments on the long side. But certain consumers such as refiners, having low inventories in the expectation of lower prices, had to keep coming back to the cash market to buy for their current requirements. So prices held up higher and longer than anyone might have expected. Lower oil prices were so obvious that they didn't happen until years after the idea became popular. And many traders on the short side got creamed as Futures rose to cash.

Under normal circumstances trading with the Wellspring System will not be substantially affected by carrying charges, since traders are seldom held for a very long time. Nevertheless, it is useful to know how carrying charges can either increase or decrease both profits and losses.

PREMIUMS AND BULL MARKETS

When demand for any commodity increases, the price will normally start to go up unless there is a parallel increase in supply, which seldom happens. If a shortage of immediately available supply develops, the price will go up a lot. The cash price will respond most, since users have to pay up to meet their commitments. But both cash and nearby Futures prices can be pushed to a premium over the price of deferred Futures: people know that there is an immediate shortage but expect either that more supply will be available later to alleviate the shortage or that increased demand is temporary.

Frequently the expectation of a short-lived shortage is incorrect. Once a shortage develops, it is much more likely to feed on itself. Shortages create greater shortages. Users scramble to lock in supplies; hoarders stock up in anticipation of higher prices and producers, seeing a rising market, are in no hurry to deliver today what may sell for more next week.

A market where the cash and nearby Futures prices are higher than the deferred is called an inverted market, a premium market or backwardation. An inverted market is a highly reliable indicator for some of the biggest bull markets. Since inversion tends to develop fairly early in a major bull move, you should make a point of looking for developing premiums and of applying the principles that follow.

1. Only some bull markets are also inverted markets but almost all newly inverted markets result in substantial price increases, and they usually last for several months.

The weekly Copper chart in Chapter 12 (page 85) shows a powerful bull market that followed years of going sideways. The May 1987 contract went to even money with the March a month before the breakout from its trading range and the break through the third downtrend line on the weekly chart. When the break occurred, the May went to a premium over the July. Over three years later the market was still inverted.

2. Keep a record of the cash price, the nearest Futures price, the next delivery month and the spreads between them:
   a) when looking for markets having the potential for a major bull move; and
   b) when looking to sell short at the beginning of a new bear market that is still inverted.

It is sufficient to maintain these records on the basis of weekly (Friday) closing prices. It is useful to keep them for as long as a market remains inverted.

Where there are already signs of a potential bull market, a narrowing of the spread between delivery months or the movement of nearby Futures to a premium indicates an imminent upturn in price or an acceleration if the move has already started.

The charts for December 1985 and February 1986 Live Cattle show a shift from a normal to an inverted market. At the first major low in July, the December contract was trading at a discount (a normal market). By the time of the low in September, it had gone to a slight premium (an inverted market), which started increasing immediately.

3. The narrowing of spreads or the emergence of a premium do not, of themselves, constitute a buy signal. You must still use other indicators to confirm that the market is in a bull trend or that a bull market is emerging (Chapters 7, 8, 9), along with trading formations and entry rules (Chapters 4,5).

4. Although the nearby contract will look expensive compared with the deferred, don't think that you will get a larger move by buying the deferred at a lower price.

You can be certain of the current shortage, but you don't know how long it will last. Therefore, go with the leader! It is immediate, intense demand that has produced an inverted market; thus the greatest price movement will be in cash and the nearby contract. If the shortage persists, as it did with Copper, you can continue to trade the market by rolling your contracts forward when the time comes. That is likely to produce far more profit than buying deferred contracts.

In an extreme case, nearby Futures can go up and deferred Futures can go down. The charts for July and October 1986 Cotton on page 116 provide a dramatic example of how the nearby and deferred Futures diverged in response to supply and demand pressures, in this case caused by the difference between crop years.

5. Be very cautious about selling an inverted market short.

A market can make a top and establish a full-fledged bear market while remaining

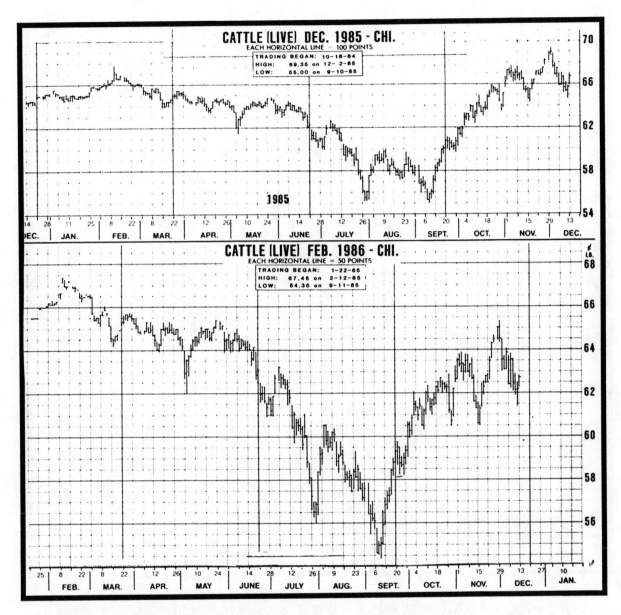

CATTLE (LIVE) DEC. 1985 - CHI.
EACH HORIZONTAL LINE = 100 POINTS

TRADING BEGAN: 10-16-84
HIGH: 69.35 on 12- 2-85
LOW: 55.00 on 9-10-85

1985

CATTLE (LIVE) FEB. 1986 - CHI.
EACH HORIZONTAL LINE = 50 POINTS

TRADING BEGAN: 1-22-85
HIGH: 67.45 on 2-12-85
LOW: 54.35 on 9-11-85

inverted. However, an inversion always shows greater buying pressure for nearby delivery than for deferred delivery. Therefore, unless there are known differences in supply and demand fundamentals between contracts, such as a new harvest, there is a risk of price heading back toward the high, or beyond it, as long as the inversion exists. The selloff in Copper from the high at $1.46 suggested that a durable top was in place. However, the continuing inversion warned of the buying pressure to come, which took price to new highs and kept it high for far longer than anyone who didn't know about the inverted market might have believed possible.

When selling short in an inverted market, make sure that most indicators clearly confirm a top. Also, continue to keep a record of the spreads between cash, the nearby and deferred contracts to monitor demand pressures. Providing that the indicators

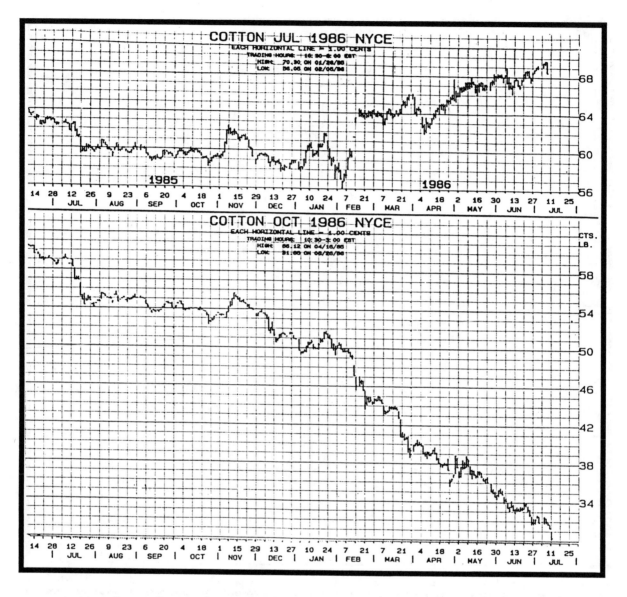

unequivocally confirm a short sale, this is one case where you should generally sell the nearby contract, even if it's stronger: it has further to fall.

6. Although not necessarily related directly to inverted markets, the charts for cash prices often give advance notice of forthcoming changes in direction. A cash market will often stop going up several weeks before the top in Futures and will often stop going down well before the bottom in Futures.

The charts for cash Sugar and March 1986 Futures show how the cash market bottomed out a full two months before Futures, thus setting up an alert for a possible market to trade.

116

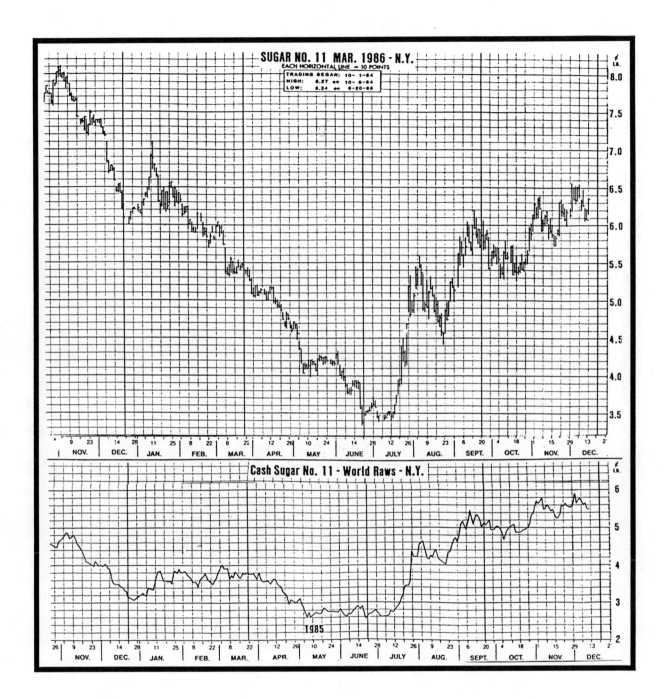

SUGAR NO. 11 MAR. 1986 - N.Y.
EACH HORIZONTAL LINE = 10 POINTS

TRADING BEGAN:	10- 1-84
HIGH:	8.27 on 10- 8-84
LOW:	3.34 on 6-20-85

Cash Sugar No. 11 - World Raws - N.Y.

1985

Chapter 16

Commitments Of Traders

Remarkable as it may seem, information is published that tells you where the smart money is going. All that's required to profit from it is a little guidance on where to find it and what to look for.

Twice a month, the Commodity Futures Trading Commission publishes data called Commitments of Traders (CoT). It indicates the distribution of various categories of traders who are long and short at the end of the reporting period and how these positions have changed since the last report.

You should obtain this information as soon after publication as possible. A good source in the format that you need is the Futures Chart Service published by Commodity Research Bureau.

The principles for interpreting the CoT are straightforward.

1. Large speculators are generally right about the major direction of markets, particularly when they establish a major commitment.

   A major commitment consists of a net position of ten percentage points or more on one side of the market or the other.

2. Small traders are generally wrong about the major direction of markets, particularly when they have a pronounced weighting of positions on one side of the market.

   This is a less reliable indicator than the one for large speculators. It has to be tempered with the knowledge that small traders have a bias toward the long side of the market.

3. Hedgers have a greater likelihood of being right than wrong, but not sufficiently so to serve as a useful indicator.

4. The strongest CoT configuration occurs when large speculators and hedgers trade heavily in the same direction, while small traders are positioned heavily in the opposite direction.

5. Look for significant shifts in CoT from one reporting period to the next. Changes in sentiment are as important as net positions, since they show the movement of money into markets.

COMMITMENTS OF TRADERS—LARGE HEDGERS, SPECULATORS AND SMALL TRADERS											
Open Interest Positions Shown in Percent (Rounded) as of November 30, 1985											
	LARGE HEDGERS				LARGE SPECULATORS				SMALL TRADERS			
MARKETS	Long	Short	Net	Δ	Long	Short	Net	Δ	Long	Short	Net	Δ
Cattle (Live)	24	39	-15	-3	9	4	+5	+6	63	54	+9	-2
Cocoa	80	80	0	-2	5	7	-2	-1	15	13	+2	+3
Coffee	30	64	-34	-6	21	3	+18	+6	49	32	+17	+2
Copper	26	78	-52	-8	26	2	+24	+11	44	17	+27	-4
Corn	52	58	-6	-6	7	2	+5	+2	36	34	+2	+5
Cotton	44	58	-14	+3	9	3	+6	-3	42	34	+8	0
Crude Oil (N.Y.)	65	58	+7	-3	11	15	-4	-1	21	25	-4	+2
Gold (Comex)	65	60	+5	-5	5	7	-2	+2	22	25	-3	+3
Heating Oil #2	47	63	-16	-1	12	7	+5	-3	39	28	+11	+4
Hogs	9	16	-7	-5	24	9	+15	+1	56	64	-8	+5
Leaded Gas (N.Y.)	62	68	-6	-2	10	4	+6	+5	27	26	+1	-3
Lumber	27	45	-18	-7	7	9	-2	-7	60	40	+20	+15
Orange Juice	23	58	-35	-6	10	7	+3	-9	64	33	+31	+14
Platinum	16	66	-50	+1	29	5	+24	+12	52	27	+25	-14
Pork Bellies	17	19	-2	+2	16	25	-9	+6	62	51	+11	-8
Silver (Comex)	45	67	-22	-4	12	10	+2	+5	39	19	+20	-1
Soybeans	39	43	-4	+11	5	10	-5	-9	51	41	+10	-1
Soybean Meal	45	50	-5	+19	7	4	+3	-8	45	44	+1	-11
Soybean Oil	44	28	+16	-4	1	6	-5	+3	47	58	-11	+1
Sugar "11"	44	83	-39	-1	11	*	+11	+1	44	16	+28	+1
Wheat (CHI)	30	30	0	+20	14	8	+6	-4	50	55	-5	-15
Wheat (K.C.)	52	48	+4	+20	3	1	+2	-8	40	47	-7	-13
Wheat (Minn)	69	64	+5	+6	1	0	+1	+1	27	34	-7	-8
Euro $	64	67	-3	+3	5	7	-2	-4	24	20	+4	0
T-Bills (90 Days)	52	72	-20	-2	6	2	+4	-2	40	24	+16	+4
T-Bonds	58	57	+1	+6	9	10	-1	-5	26	25	+1	-1
T-Notes	83	73	+10	+4	5	12	-7	-3	9	12	-3	0
NYSE Composite	25	10	+15	+4	23	29	-6	+7	40	49	-9	-11
S&P 500	54	40	+14	+11	6	15	-9	-2	39	44	-5	-8
Value Line	18	21	-3	+9	19	31	-12	+2	60	46	+14	-12
British Pound	48	73	-25	+1	13	8	+5	-2	37	18	+19	-1
Deutsche Mark	27	80	-53	+4	28	2	+26	+5	44	17	+27	-9
Japanese Yen	25	85	-60	+9	31	1	+30	-2	42	11	+31	-5
Swiss Franc	23	77	-54	+2	27	3	+24	+2	48	17	+31	-3

120

The chart on page 120 for the CoT figures published by CRB shows its tabulation of the data as of November 30, 1985. Look at the net positions for large speculators and their percentage change from the previous month.

The table below breaks out the Futures markets in which the large speculators held major positions (net positions of ten percentage points or more), together with prices three months later, the subsequent highs or lows to July 1986 and the month in which they were made.

Commitments of Large Speculators as of November 30, 1985

Large Long Positions	Net (%)	Change (%) (from Oct. 31)	Price Dec. 13, 1985	Price March 1986	High Price
Coffee	+18	+6	195.96	260.00	288.00 (Jan)
Copper	+24	+11	64.20	68.00	68.00 (Mar)
Live Hogs	+15	+1	47.55	46.00	62.00 (June)
Platinum	+24	+12	332.70	440.00	455.00 (July)
Sugar	+11	+1	6.35	9.60	9.60 (Mar)
D-Mark	+26	+5	39.62	45.00	46.75 (Apr)
Japanese Yen	+30	-2	49.23	58.00	63.00 (July)
Swiss Franc	+24	+2	47.85	55.00	57.00 (July)
Large Short Positions					
S&P 500	-9	-2	210.00	243.00	253.00 (June)
Value Line Index	-12	+2	217.95	240.00	248.00 (June)

Note that the large speculators were right on the major direction for eight out of the ten Futures markets in which they held large net positions on November 30, 1985. The exceptions were for the two Stock Index Futures.

The chart for July 1986 Platinum on page 122 shows the behavior of that market during the seven-month period after a reading of +24% net long for large speculators in November 1985 and +12% in October. The hedgers, however, had been 50% net short, presumably reflecting forward sales by mining companies, rather than users hedging inventory. While small traders had a net long position of 25%, they baled out very early in the new bull market, thus demonstrating the point that small traders are generally wrong about the major direction. Incidentally, after July 1986, Platinum gathered speed, as occurs with some of the best bull markets, and topped out at $676 in September 1986.

If you have access to the CFTC's data for CoT, you can compile it readily in the format used by CRB. Note that the CFTC's terminology differs from CRB's. The CFTC's Non-Commercials are called Large Speculators by CRB; Commercials are called Large Hedgers and Non-Reportable Positions are called Small Traders.

The important information is the percentage of all positions held long and the percentage of all positions held short by each category of trader. If, for example, the Large

Speculators hold 10% of all long positions and 20% of all short positions, they are net short 10%. CRB's chart also shows the change in net positions from the preceding period, with plus meaning an increase in net long positions and minus an increase in net short positions.

It is remarkable how the CoT figures can sometimes alert you to a trade having enormous potential that you might otherwise overlook. They can also keep you in markets where there is far more potential for a trade than you might have expected. And they can help to keep you out of markets likely to go sideways or, worst of all, backfire with a substantial move in the direction opposite to what you might otherwise have expected. For example, you might believe that a major top is forming, based on other indicators. But if the large speculators have a substantial net long position when you expect the beginning of a new bear market, prices will likely remain high or go higher rather than go down, as you expect. Similarly, markets are unlikely to advance far out of an apparently low level if the large speculators are heavily net short.

While the CoT figures provide an excellent indicator of major trends, you cannot rely on them in isolation from our other indicators. They are independent of the Wellspring System's approaches to timing entries and exits. Even when the large speculators are 100% right about the market, they are prepared to live through much larger retracements than we find advisable. Also, like any indicator, the CoT figures can be 100% wrong, as shown by the example of the Stock Index Futures. Their reliability approaches 80% when they deliver a strong signal. But that still leaves one in five times when markets fail to move in the direction that the large speculators' net positions suggest.

In conclusion, while large speculators can be wrong, like everyone else, their record of being right is sufficiently reliable to make the CoT an important indicator. Many of the best trades are confirmed by this indicator and relatively few are negated by it.

Chapter 17

Cycles

Run your finger over almost any Futures chart, going from left to right over the waves from highs to lows. It should be apparent that there is generally a certain regularity to the waves.

Does this regularity occur with enough exactitude to be useful?

Yes — but not without major limitations and much erratic behavior.

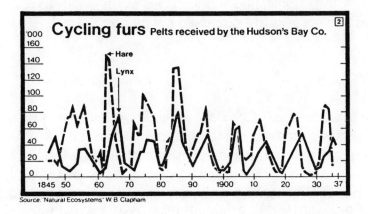

The chart illustrating the number of lynx and snowshoe hare pelts received by the Hudson's Bay Company over a period of 90 years shows a regular cycle of about nine years. This cycle is explained by fluctuations in food supply (*The Economist*, April 26, 1986). As the population of hares rises, the vegetation becomes more sparse; the population therefore declines so the vegetation recovers, and so on. The number of lynx is also controlled by their food supply — the hares.

This, however, does not explain the regularity of a pelt cycle lasting nine years or the fact that other commodities often have a longer term cycle that runs for about nine years, as measured from plenty to plenty.

There are many other regular cycles in nature and in life generally. For example, there is some evidence for a long-wave economic cycle, often known as the Kondratieff cycle, as well as an interest-rate cycle, averaging 54 years. It may be more than coincidental that there is a longer-term eclipse cycle lasting 54 years and comprised of three 19-year eclipse cycles or saros cycles. In addition, it takes the moon 8.8 years to travel from its apogee in relation to the earth (its most distant point) to its perigee (its nearest point), and another 8.8 years to return to its apogee. There may be a relationship between these forces and the frequent occurrence of commodity price cycles varying between about eight and ten years.

We know that thousands of years ago people living in many parts of the world developed knowledge of astronomical cycles that far exceeds what is generally known today except by those working directly in such fields as astrophysics. We don't know why this knowledge was pursued so assiduously, since it far surpasses any level normally required for setting a year-long calendar to use for planting crops. Cycles and their inter-relationships are part of the mystery of the astronomers of the Sumerians, the Aztecs, the ancient Chinese and the builders of Stonehenge.

For the purpose of trading Futures, it is enough to know that the regularity of cycles justifies paying attention to them. Even the greatest skeptic must acknowledge the cyclical fluctuations of the seasons, which obviously affect production and consumption cycles, and are related to astronomical variation — the movement of the earth.

As the above examples suggest, smaller cycles exist within larger cycles. We look at longer-term cycles to find markets to trade and at shorter term cycles for entering and liquidating trades. A table indicating many cycles is on page 132. Cycles involving equinoxes, solstices and eclipses are discussed in Chapter 18.

LONG-TERM CYCLES

The long-term chart for cash Corn shows cycles relating to price, as discussed in Chapter 6. It also shows cycles relating to time, marked on the bottom of the chart from low to low, without regard to the amplitude of price fluctuations. Cycles are always marked from low to low, since they occur with much greater consistency than highs.

Between 1921 and 1987, there were seven major cycles over a period of 65 years (with the last low coming in early 1987). Although these cycles lasted from seven years to 12 years, they averaged 9.3 years. You therefore cannot arbitrarily look to buy Corn nine years after a major low. But you can start looking for a possible major low to occur some time after seven years have elapsed since the previous nine-year low, using major long-term price targets as a rough guide to suggest when a low might be in place.

While a period of approximately nine years generally accommodates fluctuations in price between the fat-cat zone and the bankruptcy zone, other clearly identifiable cycles recur within this cycle. Longer-term cycles typically subdivide into smaller cycles of one-half or one-third of the longer one. Sometimes both half cycles and one-third cycles can co-exist, overlapping each other. For example, a market may have a four to five year cycle as well as one of about three years. Even when they are working with perfect regularity, they cannot bottom simultaneously more than once every eight to ten years.

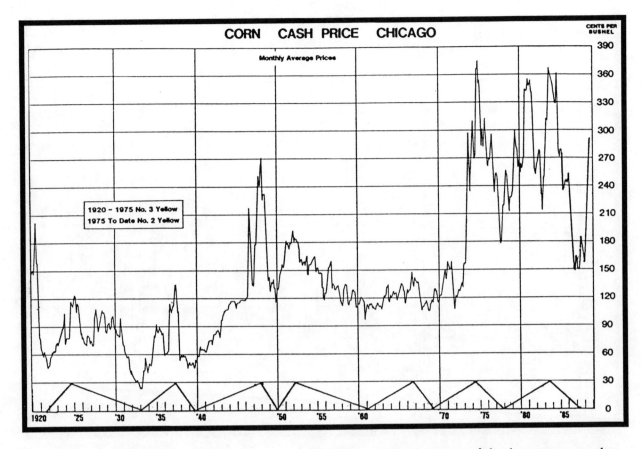

CORN CASH PRICE CHICAGO

Monthly Average Prices

1920 – 1975 No. 3 Yellow
1975 To Date No. 2 Yellow

CENTS PER BUSHEL

The best trades generally occur in markets having the majority of the long-term cycles working in the same direction. When several longer-term cycles bottom or crest simultaneously, the subsequent move is usually very powerful and sustained. But when longer-term cycles are not all working in the same direction, price movements may be erratic.

It is useful to mark long-term cycles on the weekly charts and shorter cycles on the daily charts. When cycles are open to ambiguous interpretation, which is fairly frequent, be prepared to use dotted lines and to revise your interpretation in light of later price action.

The following are typical longer and intermediate length cycles which often occur within an eight to ten year cycle:

4-5 years (half cycle)
35-40 months (three year or one-third cycle)
1 year (averaging about 46 weeks)
1/2 year (averaging about 23 weeks)

The cash chart for Pork Bellies on page 128 shows its ten-year cycle on the top and a shorter cycle averaging 41 months (the one-third cycle) on the bottom. It illustrates how the great ten-year swing in Pork Bellies is itself comprised of huge swings. In practical trading terms, three major uptrends and three major downtrends during a ten-year cycle present the possibility of six major long-term trades, three on the long side and three on the short side of the market.

127

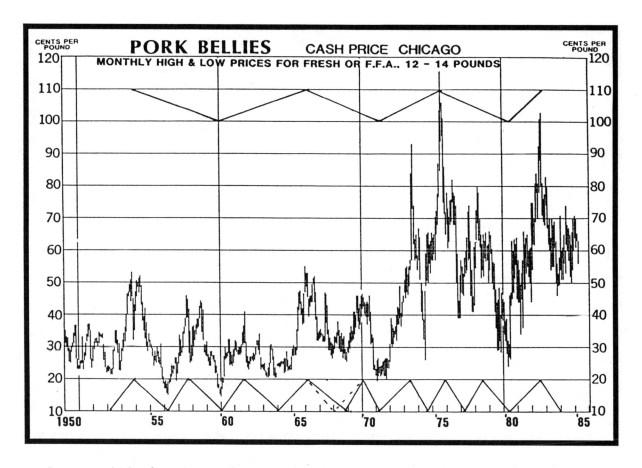

In general, the first 41-month cycle out of a ten-year low will produce a powerful bull market. The market, after all, is normally coming out of the bankruptcy zone after supplies have become very tight. Look at the tremendous thrust with which the cash Bellies market came out of the coincident ten-year and 41-month cyclical lows in 1971. The surge out of the ten-year low in 1960 was not quite so extreme: price went up by less than three times instead of more than four times.

Both of these ten-year cycles illustrate another general rule: the performance of the first 41-month cycle in a ten-year cycle suggests how the entire ten-year cycle will perform. Notice also that the highs of the ten-year cycles starting in 1960 and 1971 occurred during the second 41-month cycle. This is quite common. Finally, as can be seen, the third 41-month cycle is the most bearish, taking prices once again to the bankruptcy zone for the ten-year low.

Other markets have variations of their own. Financial markets, for example, have cycles that appear to be related in part to the routine release of certain economic and financial information. But this does not explain the regular larger cycles that these markets also have. People's actions seem to be subject to cyclical forces even when they don't know it!

SHORT AND INTERMEDIATE-TERM CYCLES

At the short end of the scale, prices generally fluctuate in cycles of about three to five weeks. These are called monthly cycles for ease of identification, despite their loose adherence to a calendar month.

In turn, the monthly cycles generally move in a larger cycle of two or more monthly cycles that end in more pronounced lows. Live Cattle, for example, have a fairly regular double monthly cycle of about nine weeks. Depending, therefore, on the amplitude of price fluctuations, a Wellspring System trade in Live Cattle might last for about two to three weeks during the up or down portion of a monthly cycle, or for six to eight weeks during the up or down portion of a double cycle.

Most markets also have annual cycles of about 45 to 70 weeks and these cycles frequently subdivide into two or three cycles of similar length.

When looking for markets to trade, there is no substitute for looking at cycles in light of their recent behavior. Sometimes a cyclical rhythm in Cattle, for instance, can shift so that more pronounced lows occur every 11 to 12 weeks, instead of about every nine weeks.

Sometimes cycles will seem to disappear, particularly in powerfully moving markets. When you can't find a cycle, assume that it is only temporarily invisible, not that its influence has ended. The next cycle low is likely to occur in the expected time-frame. Also, it is surprising how cycles move to re-establish their average duration. An unusually short cycle, for example, will frequently be followed by an unusually long one so that the overall rhythm of the market continues.

The chart for August 1989 Soybean Oil on page 130 shows six monthly cycles having a length between 16 and 45 days, with an average of 35 days. Two of these cycles combine to make a double cycle averaging nine weeks, with easily identifiable lows. In this case, Soybean Oil was in a bear market. If it were in a bull market, the lows might not be so clearly defined and the primary cycle would probably average about 11 weeks. This is because cycle lengths can vary somewhat depending on the major trend, with cycles in bull markets tending to be longer than those in bear markets. (Markets normally take longer to go up than to go down, since it takes inflows of new money to push prices higher; markets can decline on an absence of buyers and are likely to decline faster than they rise.)

The Soybean Oil chart shows how cycle theory can aid in timing entry to markets. The first sell signal on December 13 should have been viewed with skepticism. The cycle, with a likely length of about nine weeks, was only 13 days from its low on November 29. Even though the upward leg of cycles in bear markets will generally be shorter than the downward leg, only the most bearish of cycles could be expected to peak so quickly.

Although each of the second highs in the three double-monthly cycles was higher than the first, this is not necessarily the norm, particularly in bear markets. Trades on the short side entered on a lower second high have a slightly greater theoretical chance of success, since they form a small M-Formation on the daily chart. Note also the shorter duration of the run-up to the second high in each cycle. This behavior is typical of bear markets.

It is useful to count the days within monthly cycles, as shown on the Soybean Oil chart. Calendar days provide a better count than market days because money keeps on changing

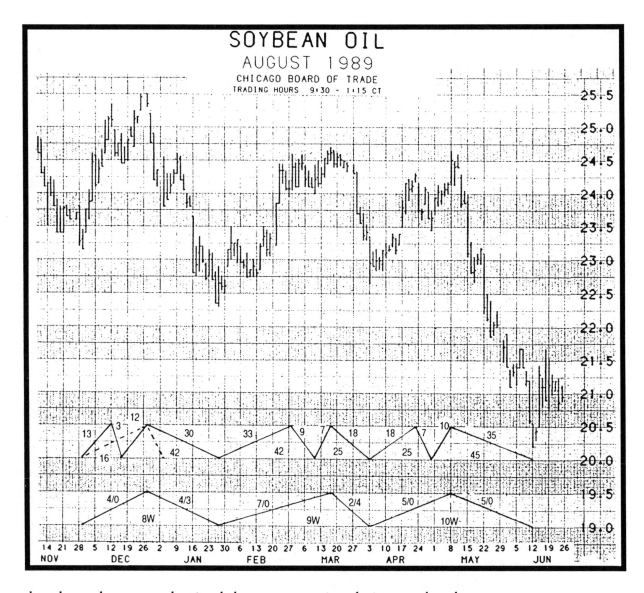

hands, and crops and animals keep on growing during weekends.

As with all indicators, cycle theory has its moments of glory and its times of tribulation. It is most useful when you start by identifying the big picture for a market to trade, particularly by using the indicators and approaches described in Chapters 6 to 12. Then look for the long-term cycles and work through to the shorter cycles.

Some traders try to use cycles as the starting point for selecting markets to trade, often aiming to pick market tops and bottoms. This approach can be disastrous. Failure to use cycles in the context of other indicators can lead to entering markets and to liquidating profitable trades far too early. Premature entry results in many unnecessary losses and premature exit in foregoing substantial profits. A market making an extended move often appeals to traders looking for a substantial profit when the market turns, tempting them to enter trades when they feel that a cycle ought to be in the right time frame for a top or a bottom. Instead, a market making an extended move in terms of price may also do so in terms of time.

In sum, use cycles as part of the discipline of waiting for the right times to get into markets and to bank profits *when other indicators also tell you to act.* Don't be impatient!

As a further guide to the exercise of patience and getting the time right, we now move to some specific times when turning points may be expected.

SELECTED CYCLES

This table lists the average length of some of the most regular cycles which have been evident in various markets. It does not purport to be complete because of variations which occur in all markets some of the time and in some markets for most of the time. The numbers in brackets indicate some benchmark lows up to April 1991 in order to help you establish your own counts of cycles.

	Long-Term Cycles (Years Unless Indicated)	Intermediate Cycles (Weeks)	Monthly Cycles (Calendar Days)
STOCK INDEXES	4 (10/90)	22 (10/90)	
INTEREST RATES			
Treasury Bills		45 (10/90), 22, 8-14	28
Eurodollars		45 (11/90), 22, 8-14	28
Treasury Bonds	10 (9/90), 3 (9/90)	45 (9/90), 22, 8-14	28
CURRENCIES			
U.S. Dollar Index		48 (2/91), 17, 13, 8	21
British Pound	4 (6/89)	37 (12/90), 26 (9/90), 8	28
Canadian Dollar		60 (1/90), 11	21
D-Mark	4 (6/89)	30 (4/91), 8	28
Japanese Yen		70 (4/90), 8	28
Swiss Franc	4 (6/89)	22 (7/91), 8	28
METALS			
Gold	9 (1985)	18 (10/90), 7-8	21
Platinum		17 (10/90), 7-8	28
Silver	9 (1986)	18 (2/91), 7-8	35
Copper		45 (1/91), 15, 7	25
PETROLEUM			
Crude & Heating Oil		30 (2/91), 15	
GRAINS, SOYBEANS			
Corn	9 (1987), 3	46 (11/90), 20	28
Wheat	9 (1986), 4 1/2	46 (1/91), 20	35
Soybeans	39, 24 mos. (8/90)	45 (1/91), 14	28
Soybean Meal		43 (1/91), 11	28
Soybean Oil		50 (1/91), 11	28
MEATS			
Feeder Cattle		47 (1/91), 9	
Live Cattle	11 & 7.5 (1985), 45 mos. (6/89)	48 (7/90), 9	
Live Hogs	36 mos.	45 (8/90), 7-14	
Pork Bellies	10 (8/89), 41 mos. (8/89)	47 (7/90), 17	35
FOODS			
Cocoa	10 (1982), 7 (12/89)	40 (8/90)	28
Coffee	20 (1981), 3 (10/89)	45 (11/90)	35
Sugar	7 (1985)	78 (5/91), 15	25
FIBERS			
Cotton		60 (3/91), 28-35	35-45

Chapter 18

Turning Points: Landmarks In Time

EQUINOXES AND SOLSTICES

Markets frequently make important turns and changes in trend that coincide with astronomical events. There is considerable evidence to support this contention, particularly for the equinoxes (equal day and night, March 21 and September 21) and the solstices (the longest and shortest days, June 21 and December 21).

These times also correspond to the changes of the seasons and the times of the greatest and smallest tides. At the equinoxes, the tides are greatest and at the solstices smallest. It is not surprising in general terms that the changing seasons coincide with changes in the way that people think about market prices. It is surprising, however, that many markets, including those having no direct connection with readily identifiable patterns of production or consumption, often turn at times close to the equinoxes and solstices.

By no means all markets make important turns at these quarter-year points, but the incidence of it happening is so overwhelming that we have to pay attention. When a major cyclical turn is expected or when price is approaching a major level of support or resistance, the market is likely to continue its current direction until the time of the quarter-year. It is likely to head for that time-frame as if drawn by a magnet, a marker buoy or a beacon. Hence a landmark in time. On arrival in the respective time-frame, the market is likely to turn within about seven days on either side of the landmark in time.

The chart for the December 1985 D-Mark on the next page shows a relentless bear market during the first three months of 1985. At the beginning of March 1985, the market began to show turbulence, suggesting a possible change in sentiment. For three weeks the market seemed to go into a period of "slack water" (the neutral period which occurs in many locations as the tide is turning). Then, on March 19, price conclusively crossed over the remaining trendlines and completed a strong trading formation buy signal by leaving an island behind. The market was on its way, having turned at the spring equinox.

The next major surge upward had its beginning with a daily upside reversal on exactly June 21. The last major upsurge shown the D-Mark chart began on September 20. With

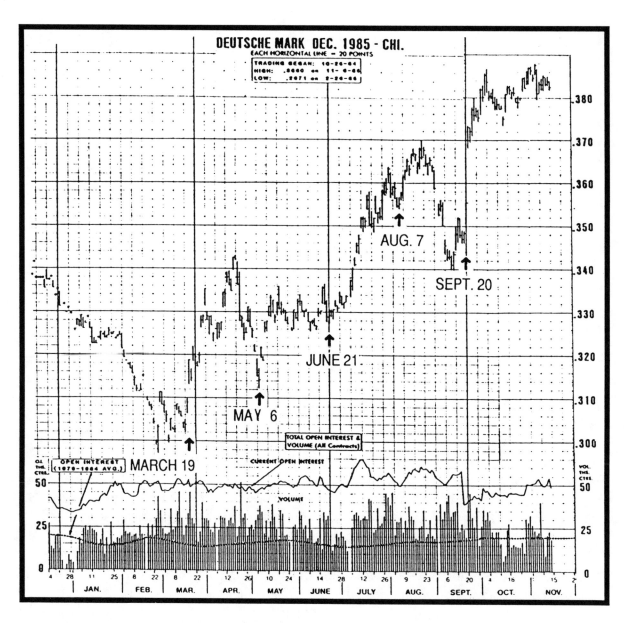

DEUTSCHE MARK DEC. 1985 - CHI.
EACH HORIZONTAL LINE = 20 POINTS

TRADING BEGAN: 10-26-84
HIGH: .3660 on 11-8-85
LOW: .2671 on 2-26-85

AUG. 7

SEPT. 20

JUNE 21

MAY 6

MARCH 19

TOTAL OPEN INTEREST & VOLUME (All Contracts)

OPEN INTEREST (1979-1984 AVG.)

CURRENT OPEN INTEREST

VOLUME

September 21 falling on a Saturday, the market couldn't get any closer to the equinox!

THE NEW MOON AND THE FULL MOON

As already noted, there is a relationship between the year's quarters and the tides, which are directly influenced by the pull of the moon. While this is a scientifically proven relationship, there is more than a coincidental relationship between the moon and human behavior, and between the moon and the movement of markets. For thousands of years, lunar influences have been thought to exert an influence on human behavior. Hence the word lunatic, or its equivalent, in many languages.

When a market turn is expected on the basis of other indicators, there is a much greater likelihood of the top or bottom occurring within one day of the New Moon or the Full Moon than any normal statistical probability might suggest. The likelihood of a turn occurring on one of these six days is sufficiently great that you should make a point of noting the lunar cycle.

While major turns can occur either at the New Moon or the Full Moon, there are certain periods which are more favorable for short-term highs and lows.

The most favorable time for a short-term *low* is during the eight-day period starting six days before the New Moon and ending one day after the New Moon (NM - 6 to NM + 1).

The most favorable time for a short-term *high* is during the seven-day period starting four days before the Full Moon and ending two days after the Full Moon (FM - 4 to FM + 2).

When looking to enter a trade, shift the entry window two days later so that a trading formation has time to be completed. Therefore:

The ideal buy signal would occur between NM - 4 and NM + 3; and

The ideal sell signal would occur between FM - 2 and FM + 4.

ECLIPSES

The effect of lunar and solar eclipses was not studied for this book. Since the Wellspring System does not lack for reliable indicators, it seemed superfluous to pursue detailed work on a phenomenon which seldom occurs. Nevertheless, there is credible evidence suggesting more of a relationship between eclipses and market turns than could reasonably be explained by coincidence. The evidence includes examples of the New York Stock Exchange making major turns within an hour of an eclipse.

Whatever the merits of studies relating astronomical forces and price-forecasting, there is an investment advisory service doing work based on this approach (Crawford Perspectives, 205 East 78th Street, New York, NY 10021). On June 30, 1990 they wrote, "Expect some major catastrophe on that last one (Lunar Eclipse squares Mars + Pluto Aug. 6), Aug. 2-7, as something explodes in a big way (may be nuclear or volcanic). Astronomically similar to Chernobyl disaster — awesome, awful but did not affect the stock market much!" (Quoted in *Barron's*, July 16, 1990.)

On August 2, 1990, Iraq invaded Kuwait!

GANN DATES

W. D. Gann, the famous trader of the early 20th Century, found that there was particular significance to certain numbers and certain days. Studies for the Wellspring System found that these numbers can be useful and that Gann's dates, particularly the equinoxes and solstices, as already discussed, often serve as important landmarks in time.

The following are Gann's key observations concerning landmarks in time:

1. There is a marked tendency for history to repeat itself on or about the anniversary of previous important market turns. Similar turns are as likely to occur several years later as just one year later.

2. There is particular significance to the number seven and its multiples, especially 49 days or seven weeks from an earlier high or low.

3. 42 to 45 days is an interval that can be significant, representing one-eighth of a year and one-eighth of 360 degrees in a circle. Multiples of 42 to 45 days such as 90 and 135 days (approximately) can also be important.

4. Including the equinoxes and solstices, the most important calendar days in Gann's year, which begins on March 21, are:

Date	Significance
May 5	1/8 year or 6 1/2 weeks (45 days)
June 21	1/4 year or 13 weeks (summer solstice)
August 5	3/8 year or 19 1/2 weeks
September 21	1/2 year or 26 weeks (fall equinox)
November 8	5/8 year or 32 1/2 weeks
December 21	3/4 year or 39 weeks (winter solstice)
February 4	7/8 year or 45 1/2 weeks
March 21	1 year or 52 weeks (spring equinox)

Look for potential market turns to occur within plus or minus seven calendar days of these dates. As well as the equinox and solstice turning points already mentioned, a very important low occurred in the D-Mark on Monday, May 6, the closest possible market day to the 1/8 year landmark in time. A smaller low occurred on August 7, two days after the 3/8 year landmark in time.

USING TURNING POINTS AND CYCLES

The chart for August 1989 Soybean Oil shows how cycles, lunar phases and other landmarks in time can be used together.

In looking for a place to go short, the ideal time to do so, in theory, would be at the crest of the double monthly cycle and within the time frame of the Full Moon (FM - 2 to FM + 4) as well as one of Gann's dates. The first double monthly cycle high occurred on December 23. This date coincided with the Full Moon and was two days after the winter solstice, thus bringing together two coincident timing indicators. The low for the move occurred on January 26, eight days before February 4, the Gann day representing 7/8 of

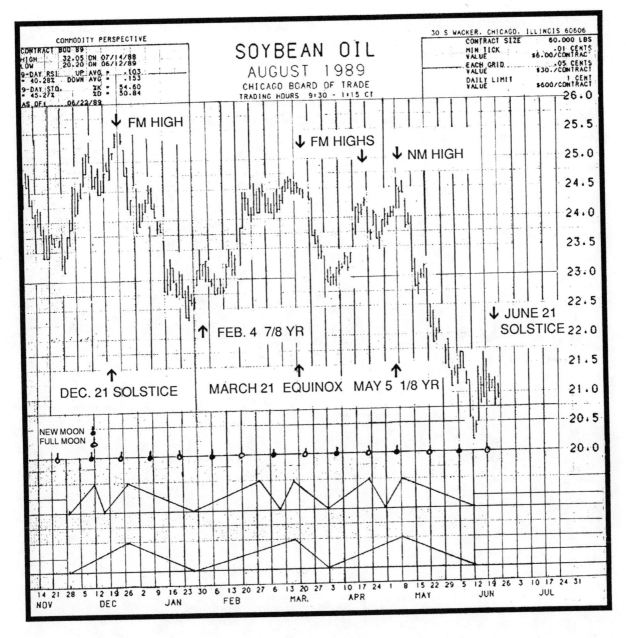

the year, and one day outside the ideal time frame.

    The cyclical high for the second double monthly cycle occurred on March 16, five days before the equinox. It came six days before the Full Moon, or two days early for the ideal time frame.

    For the third double monthly cycle, the initial monthly high occurred on the day of the Full Moon. The double monthly cycle high occurred one day after the New Moon and one day after the Gann date for 1/8 year. From there, the market continued sliding until the New Moon time window nearest to the summer solstice.

    You are fully entitled to be skeptical about the concept of landmarks in time acting to draw markets like a magnet and then to serve as turning points. However, you are almost certain to increase your trading profits measurably by marking your diary with lunar phases and Gann dates, and by taking them into consideration when making trading decisions. They should help to set you up days or even weeks in advance of possible entries or exits from trades.

The point about landmarks in time is not that *every* one of them is likely to produce a turn in the market. It is that signals occurring at an ideal time have a much enhanced probability of being successful.

Chapter 19

Mathematical Indicators And Market Sentiment

The widespread use of the computer has encouraged the development of an ever-increasing number of mathematical indicators requiring daily or weekly computation. Calculation is done easily by computer, although some of them are simple enough to do manually for a few markets.

All mathematical indicators seek insights into price performance that may not be evident from daily and weekly bar charts. Several of these indicators provide information about when a market is losing its strength and when it might turn. In particular, two widely available indicators work well with the Wellspring System's other indicators: the Relative Strength Index (RSI) and stochastics. A third indicator, moving averages, is not recommended but is discussed because of its widespread and unjustified popularity.

RELATIVE STRENGTH INDEX (RSI) AND STOCHASTICS

The RSI and stochastics show momentum and are based on the idea that market momentum or internal strength leads price. Therefore, the indicators move in the same direction as price as long as the momentum of the market is maintained but will usually make a top or bottom before price does.

The August 1989 Soybean Oil chart on the next page includes both the RSI and stochastics. The %D (Percentage of Deviation) stochastic is a smoothed or lagging version of the %K stochastic. Some traders use a crossover of the two to confirm market turns, although this is not, by itself, a very reliable indicator.

Notice that the %D stochastic topped each time that it reached about 80 and that the RSI topped at about 70. Both have scales from 0 to 100. At these levels, the market is overbought in the sense that momentum has reached a level of potential exhaustion. This suggests that price may also be nearing its high.

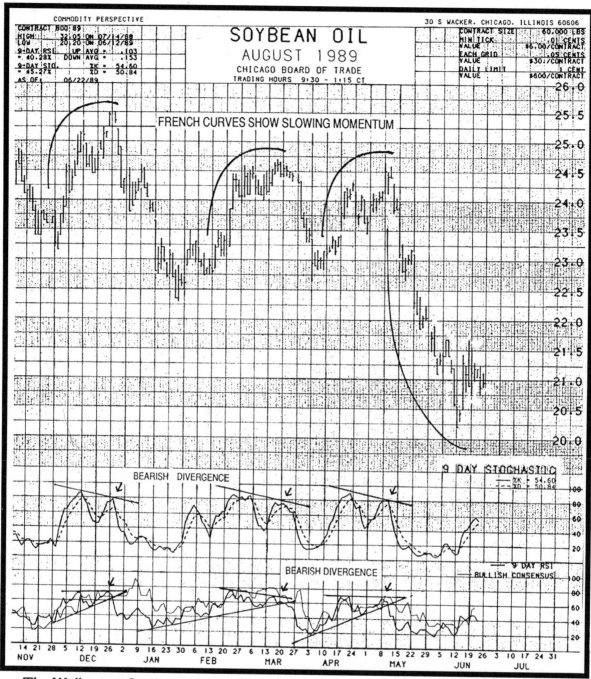

FRENCH CURVES SHOW SLOWING MOMENTUM

9 DAY STOCHASTIC

BEARISH DIVERGENCE

BEARISH DIVERGENCE

9 DAY RSI
BULLISH CONSENSUS

The Wellspring System uses the RSI and stochastics as a flashing amber light, signaling that price action may be about to change when they approach or reach overbought or oversold territory. At these levels, pay attention to other indicators that may suggest entry to a new trade or liquidation of an existing one.

In a bull market, look for an entry to go long when the RSI and stochastics are oversold. In a bear market, look for an entry to go short when the RSI and stochastics are overbought.

When holding a long position and the RSI and stochastics are overbought, or when holding a short position in oversold territory, move the stop closer in accordance with Stop Rule 5 (Chapter 13) and be prepared to liquidate the trade.

140

Note, however, that neither the RSI nor stochastics can be used to indicate market turns in *strongly trending* markets. You should not liquidate a trade until a signal comes through to do so. A strongly trending market can stay overbought or oversold far longer than you might expect. Soybean Oil was in a major bear market and both the RSI and stochastics not only overshot the oversold level on the way down, but they stayed in deeply oversold territory for over three weeks while price plunged from 23¢ to 20.2¢.

Negative divergence often occurs when the momentum of a market begins to weaken. When the RSI and stochastics turn down while price continues to rise, there is bearish divergence. When they turn up while price continues to decline, there is bullish divergence. The Soybean Oil chart shows bearish divergence. Stochastics peaked before price at the the three tops; the RSI also demonstrates bearish divergence, though not so emphatically.

This example illustrates the principle that bearish divergence in a bear market puts extra current through the amber light flashing a potential market turn, as does bullish divergence in a bull market.

Negative divergence can also be useful as a guide when looking to close out profitable positions in a runaway bull market or a collapsing bear market. The momentum will start to go out of the move well before it ends. The collapse in the price in Soybean Oil during May and June ended only after stochastics and the RSI had made higher lows. (After the low in June the market made another significant rally, not shown on this chart.)

Both the RSI and stochastics, but particularly the RSI, can develop patterns which appear only later, or not at all, on the bar chart. Watch for chart patterns such as M and W-Formations, head and shoulders, triangles, support and resistance, and trendlines. The RSI for Soybean Oil shows how breaks in its trendlines confirmed breaks in price in late December and early May, and slightly led price in March.

The RSI and stochastics, like all mathematical indicators, are useful only when updated daily with the bar charts so that the changing market conditions which they portray can be seen before they occur in price. It is preferable to do the calculations by computer; market software packages generally are programmed to do this. The daily numbers may also be available from a quotation service, if you have access to one. In that case, check whether the time period used to calculate the numbers is the same as that used on your charts. If it is different, the general picture will be the same, but you will require a new set of parameters for overbought and oversold levels.

If you wish to do the calculations manually (time-consuming for more than a few markets) or to program your computer to do the job, here are the formulas:

The Nine-Day RSI

$$RS = \frac{\text{Average of previous 9 days closes up}}{\text{Average of previous 9 days closes down}}$$

$$RSI = 100 - \left[\frac{100}{1 + RS} \right]$$

Closes up means the closing price on a day when the closing price was higher than the previous day's close, and vice versa for closes down.

Nine-Day Stochastics

This formula is used by Commodity Perspective and is plotted on its charts. It calculates momentum based on the rate of change in the daily high, low and closing prices.

$$\text{Raw Stochastic Value} = \frac{100 \times (C - L9)}{(H9 - L9)}$$

C is the latest close, L9 is the lowest low for the last 9 days and H9 is the highest high for the same 9 days.

Commodity Perspective plots two smooth 3-day moving averages, %K and %D, according to the following formulas:

%K = 2/3 previous %K + 1/3 Raw Stochastic Value
%D = 2/3 previous %D + 1/3 new %K

If you are unable to update the RSI and stochastics, you can frequently get a fair idea of how they might be performing by using a rule of thumb when looking at the daily bar charts. A market that is maintaining momentum should extend each price surge at least as far as the previous one. Markets in which momentum is flagging will often begin to curve. The Soybean Oil chart shows how French curves drawn around tops indicate slowing momentum. Notice how the RSI and stochastics performed as momentum slowed and price began to curve.

The usefulness of the RSI and stochastics increases with the length of the record for a specific contract, as well as with personal experience in using them generally. You will find, for example, that they have different identifiable characteristics in different Futures markets.

MOVING AVERAGES

Moving averages may be calculated easily by averaging the closing prices for any length of time, such as five days, five weeks or 25 weeks. They therefore smooth out erratic price behavior and attempt to distinguish the real trend from transitory market direction.

Most chart services plot moving averages using several time periods. Many traders use them as a signal to buy when price moves above an average and to sell when price moves below it.

Despite their popularity, moving averages are a snare and a delusion. Price crossing, say, a ten-day moving average might deliver the maximum profit one time, while the next trade might require a 40-day moving average to work.

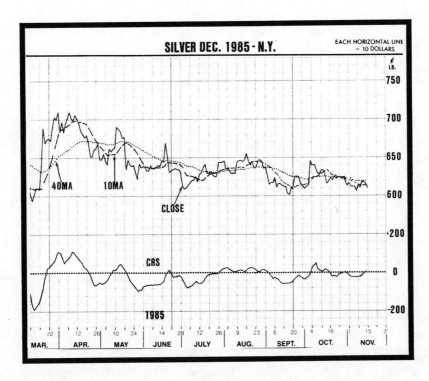

The December 1985 Silver chart shows how badly you can get chewed up by trading only with moving average crossovers. Price (represented by the solid line showing closing prices) crossed over the 40-day weighted moving average 15 time during a nine-month period but never followed through once for a worthwhile trade.

Even as a trend indicator, moving averages don't necessarily work well. Because they are based on old data, they are apt to tell you what you already know from other indicators — that the trend has changed.

MARKET SENTIMENT

Market sentiment refers to the degree of bullishness or bearishness of traders towards a specific market. Several commercial firms measure sentiment in various markets by polling market advisers, both those employed by large investment dealers and independent advisers. Some chart services plot this data. For example, Bullish Consensus (published by Hadady Corp., 309 - 61 South Lake Avenue, Pasadena CA 91101) is shown on the bottom of the August 1989 Soybean Oil chart (page 140). This chart plots the percentage of advisers whose view of the market is bullish. *Barron's* also reports market sentiment figures for the stock market, U.S. Treasury Bonds and Eurodollars.

The best trending markets generally move with a certain level of skepticism. A steady bull market will generally move, therefore, without excessive bullish sentiment, a steady bear market without excessive bearish sentiment.

Ideally, Bullish Consensus figures fluctuate between about 40% and 70% during the intermediate stages of a major move, as they also do when a market is moving sideways. The band does not extend an equal amount either side of the 50% mid-point. This is because of the pronounced bias of small traders and their advisers toward the long side of the market. In a persistent bull market, Bullish Consensus will generally fluctuate in the upper half of the range between 40 and 70%, with price action reinforced by traders following their advisers. In a persistent bear market, Bullish Consensus will generally fluctuate in the lower half of this range.

At the extremities, market sentiment serves as an important contrary indicator. When too many people become excited about trading in the same direction, the greater fool theory may take over. This theory states that a market can continue moving in the same direction simply as long as it continues to do so, regardless of the supply and demand fundamentals. Finally, however, every last enthusiast is satisfied and the market turns, often violently. It is no coincidence that the majority of advisers continue to be wrong, time after time, at important turns, since they too become emotionally involved in an apparent trend.

Above 70%, the long side of the market may be too popular to be complacent about a bull market. Above 80% there is a high probability of a sudden sharp decline. The corresponding figures to warn of a possible upturn are 20% to 40%.

On the relatively rare occasions when Bullish Consensus reaches toward 80% in what we would designate a bear market, there may be a prime opportunity to go short. Such was the case during December, March and May in the August 1989 Soybean Oil contract. Similarly, in a designated bull market, there may be a prime buying opportunity when Bullish Consensus reaches toward 30%.

Bullish Consensus can act like the mathematical indicators to give advance warning of an impending turn. Thus, a higher high in price coinciding with a declining Bullish Consensus may constitute the kind of negative divergence that warns of an approaching downturn. Eagerness to buy is waning.

Market sentiment is not in itself a timing indicator. But when used in conjunction with other indicators, it can be a very valuable tool for identifying well in advance the potential for some of the biggest trades.

Like the mathematical indicators, market sentiment must be charted regularly. Also, the longer the record, the better able you are to see the trend and significant changes to it when they occur. Market sentiment figures, like mathematical indicators, also behave differently in different markets; therefore, with experience you can get a feel for interpreting current data in the light of previous behavior.

Chapter 20

Volume and Open Interest

Volume and open interest occasionally provide vital information, particularly about exhaustion tops and bottoms, and major changes of trend. Generally, though, they act as secondary indicators, providing confirmation of information available from other indicators.

Volume and open interest are plotted by many chart services and can be updated easily. The figures reported in newspapers are for two days earlier while the numbers reported by on-line quotation services are for the previous day. Although the figures are reported by contract month, it is the totals which are charted.

The interpretation of volume and open interest is different for bull and bear markets, and these indicators are easily misinterpreted. Therefore, the information that you need to interpret them is described in concise, usable rules.

VOLUME IN BULL MARKETS

1. Days when price goes up should have heavier volume; days when price goes down should have lighter volume.

2. When price retraces and volume dries up, look for a place to buy; the advance should resume soon.

3. Highs made on lower volume than occurred at previous highs suggest that buying pressure is abating. Negative divergence gives warning of a potential top but doesn't help with timing: peaks in volume can occur long before peaks in price.

4. Where a second or third top in price occurs at approximately the same level as the preceding top and the volume is lower, the market is probably preparing to change direction.

5. When there is a shift from heavier volume on up days to heavier volume on down days, the chances are that the market is turning. If the shift is pronounced, there may be a substantial move down.

VOLUME IN BEAR MARKETS

In bear markets, volume should behave the opposite to the way it behaves in bull markets.

1. Days when price goes down should have heavier volume; days when price goes up should have lighter volume.

2. When price retraces and volume dries up, look for a place to go short; the decline should resume soon.

3. Lows made on lower volume than occurred at previous lows suggest that selling pressure is abating. Negative divergence gives warning of a potential bottom. Unlike negative divergence in a bull market, it is a more useful guide to timing, particularly when there are selling climaxes.

4. Where a second or third low in price occurs at approximately the same level as the preceding low and the volume is lower, the market is probably preparing to change direction.

5. When there is a shift from heavier volume on down days to heavier volume on up days, the chances are that the market is turning. If the shift is pronounced, there may be a substantial move up.

The chart for February 1986 Pork Bellies shows the rules for volume in action. Note the relatively high volume at the high in March compared with the lower volume at the high in June, prior to the major selloff. Also note that at the bear market low in August and September, there was some shift from heavier volume on down days to heavier volume on up days. As well, volume was generally lower (drying up) at the low price levels in September.

OPEN INTEREST

Open interest is the total number of outstanding contracts, each consisting of one buyer and one seller. Although the total fluctuates during the trading day, the number of contracts outstanding at the close of business is the reported figure.

It is important to check the open interest in markets that you are considering trading. As a general rule, there should be a total open interest of not less than 5,000 contracts,

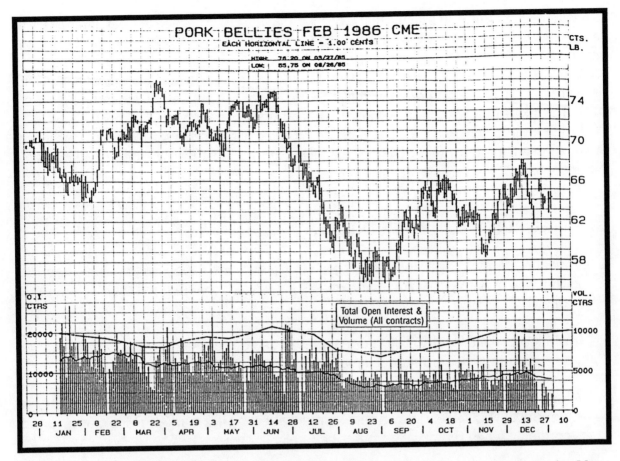

PORK BELLIES FEB 1986 CME
EACH HORIZONTAL LINE = 1.00 CENTS
HIGH: 76.20 ON 03/27/85
LOW: 55.75 ON 08/26/85

Total Open Interest & Volume (All contracts)

and not less than 3,000 contracts in the specific contract month that you might trade. You will notice that in most markets open interest is high in only a few of the nearer months. The most actively traded month is almost always preferable to trade. When considering a market having a minimum level of open interest, also check the volume figures to see whether there is a reasonable level of daily trading.

One theory about open interest states that the commercials, specifically traders such as miners, growers and owners of the actuals, in part perform the role of market-maker in providing liquidity in markets. Their actions can therefore have a substantial effect on open interest levels. They may be prepared, for example, to take the short side of the market when there is an imbalance of buying pressure. As already mentioned, the majority of the general public has a pronounced bias toward trading the long side.

A short hedger does not lose money by taking the short side of a rising market in the same sense that a speculator loses money. Hedge sales lock in prices and protect sellers against the possibility that their forthcoming production or their current inventory may sell at lower prices later on.

Bull markets often occur with the large hedgers heavily net short, according to the Commitments of Traders (CoT) figures. Evidently, the commercials are prepared to assume short positions or add to them but only at steadily rising prices. When the commercials foresee a top, however, it is likely that they will want to add to their short positions more aggressively. Therefore, a bulge in open interest may reflect the trade's expectations of a break in price. On the other hand, a sudden decline in open interest may reflect the trade's expectation of yet higher prices. They act on this expectation by covering short positions.

While it is simplistic to second-guess as to who might be the participants at any given time among the turmoil of markets, it is possible to apply this general concept to a set of rules that suggest how volume and open interest may interact.

Open interest frequently says little of importance about price forecasting. But there are times when it lights up like a beacon, signaling information that may not be evident from other sources.

GENERAL RULES FOR OPEN INTEREST

1. A sudden change in open interest suggests that a significant move in price may happen soon. It is probable that the commercials have suddenly changed their view of the market.

2. A change of the order of 25% in open interest can be very significant. Small changes may simply represent routine fluctuations.

3. When open interest increases dramatically in a listless market, there may be an important but not widely known development affecting the market. Price may respond accordingly when the news becomes generally known.

COMPARISONS OF CURRENT AND FIVE-YEAR AVERAGE OPEN INTEREST

Open interest is best interpreted against a five-year moving average because it can vary seasonally. What may appear to be an important change in open interest may merely reflect seasonal variations.

1. When current open interest is much lower than the five-year average and continuing to decline, this may indicate that a new bull market is preparing to get under way.

2. When current open interest is declining and a seasonal increase would normally be expected, the market may be preparing to go higher.

3. When current open interest is increasing and a seasonal decrease would normally be expected, the market may be preparing to go lower.

OPEN INTEREST IN BULL MARKETS

1. When open interest and price increase together, the market is strong and the price should go higher.

    Increasing open interest represents both new buying and new selling, with buyers more aggressive than sellers.

2. When open interest, volume and price decline, this will usually signal a minor retracement in a strong market.

3. When open interest declines, but volume and price both increase (an unusual occurrence), the likelihood is for the market to be exceptionally strong.

4. When open interest remains relatively flat during the beginning months of a bull market, the price is likely to be heading a lot higher for some time.

    The commercials are unwilling to add to their short positions. It will be reasonably safe to buy into this market, even if the move has been under way for some time. But be cautious when open interest starts to increase substantially, indicating the arrival of too many late-coming members of the public as participants in the market.

5. A consolidation area after a surge in price may either be a resting place in a bull market or a top may be forming. If open interest continues to climb while price is leveling off, a top should be suspected. On the other hand, if open interest dips, the likelihood is for the advance to resume when the consolidation ends.

    This is an important rule, applicable to consolidations and trading ranges generally, whether a market is going up, down or sideways. It shows whether the commercials are adding to their short positions or reducing them.

OPEN INTEREST IN BEAR MARKETS

1. When open interest and price decrease together, the market is weak and should continue to work lower.

    You don't necessarily need to have higher open interest figures on down days if the market is grinding relentlessly lower.

2. When open interest increases in a rally against the trend on light volume, this is particularly bearish. You should look for a place to go short.

    The commercials are adding to their short positions.

3. When open interest increases while price declines, the market is very weak.

    New shorts are coming aggressively into the market.

4. A consolidation area after a decline may either be a resting place in a bear market or a bottom may be forming. If open interest continues to climb while price is going sideways, a further decline is likely. On the other hand, if open interest dips, the commercials may be covering their short positions in the expectation of a rally or a change of trend.

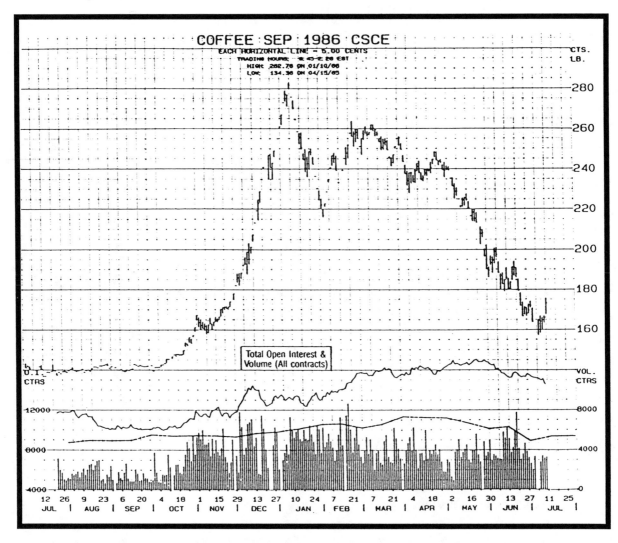

The chart for September 1986 Coffee shows typical behavior for open interest. During August and September 1985, open interest declined by nearly 20%, as the shorts covered prior to the start of the big bull market. Open interest increased throughout the bull market, peaking well after its top in price, as the general public climbed on the bandwagon and as the trade and large speculators increased short positions. The CoT figures for June 30,

1986, for example, show the small traders heavily net long and increasing their long positions substantially, while both large hedgers and large speculators were net short.

The small dips in December and March occurred in conjunction with the expiry of those months' contracts.

It is important not to try and read too much into volume and open interest data over a short period. But it can be very useful to keep an eye on them to note major aberrations when they occur and to help reach conclusions about the big picture.

Chapter 21

Stock Index Futures

Stock Index Futures have been such an excellent vehicle for trading Futures that they stand in a class of their own. They have liquidity, big trends and big swings within major trends. These factors make them the preferred trading vehicle for many professional traders. Some people trade nothing else.

The only drawback for traders starting out is that there is no "little league" starting place. You must budget for margins of $10,000 and up and, in addition, for the possibility of three consecutive $2,000 losses before even thinking of trading the Indexes (explained in Chapter 22, Capital Management). Once you have banked $10,000 to $15,000 in profits, however, you should certainly consider trading these markets.

A further reason for looking at Stock Index Futures is that helpful information exists that is not available for other markets. Here are some of the special considerations applicable to trading Index Futures:

1. The most important thing to know about the overall stock market is that it is driven by supply and demand for stocks. In turn, however, supply and demand are by no means dictated by what you might logically expect to happen.

   The main driving forces behind the stock market, in their approximate order of importance, are:

   a) Availability of money;
   b) Interest rates;
   c) Perceptions of inflation; and
   d) Fundamental economic news, including current and forecast corporate profits.

   While the overall trend of the stock market in the very long term has always been up, its fluctuations provide prime opportunities for making money on both sides of the market. Within the major long-term upward trend, there tend to be periods, amounting to about 25% of the time, when there are clear bear markets in stocks.

It is worth knowing how apparently perverse the stock market can be in relation to what you might logically expect. Consider, for instance, that during the 1950s the market averages more than doubled, while corporate profits were up less than 50%. In the 1970s, corporate profits more than doubled, while stock market averages barely broke even. From 1978 to 1985, corporate profits declined, while the market doubled.

Perceptions change over time quite as much as does reality.

2. The stock market exhibits as persistently as any other market the adage that tops are made when things look brightest and bottoms occur when it feels as if the market can never recover.

    This is where central bankers come in. Money supply is normally reined in as economic expansion approaches its top and expanded as it approaches the bottom. The stock market responds to changes in the availability of money (and interest rates) before changes in economic activity occur. The stock market tends, therefore, to be a leading indicator of economic activity, not a coincident or lagging indicator.

3. There are three prominent Stock Index Futures, each performing a slightly different function. The Major Market Index approximates most closely the Dow Jones Industrial Average and represents 20 major stocks, of which 15 are in the Dow. The Standard and Poor 500 (S&P) represents the 500 largest companies and is therefore much more broadly based than the Major Market Index. The New York Stock Exchange Composite Index represents 1.500 stocks, making it the most broadly based Index. A further trading vehicle which may become important is the Nikkei 225 Index, representing the major stocks listed in Tokyo.

4. In the big picture, there has been a consistent four-year cyclical pattern, sometimes called the Presidential Cycle. U.S. stock markets tend to make a cyclical low about the mid-point between elections and peak near the time of the election. Expectations of better times rise toward an election. On the other hand, newly elected presidents are expected to deliver strong medicine early in their term of office in order to get the bad news behind them well before the next election. While there has generally been little evidence of the actual delivery of strong medicine, money has tended to be more freely available at lower interest rates during the periods leading up to elections.

5. The Advance/Decline Line (breadth) is a better indicator of the underlying strength or weakness of the stock market than is price. It is plotted with a line showing the cumulative difference between shares going up and shares going down. It may be compiled with either weekly or daily data but there is seldom a significant difference in result, whichever method is used.

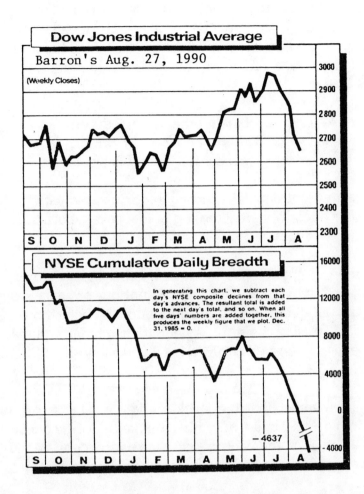

Dow Jones Industrial Average

Barron's Aug. 27, 1990

(Weekly Closes)

S O N D J F M A M J J A

3000 2900 2800 2700 2600 2500 2400 2300

NYSE Cumulative Daily Breadth

In generating this chart, we subtract each day's NYSE composite declines from that day's advances. The resultant total is added to the next day's total, and so on. When all five days' numbers are added together, this produces the weekly figure that we plot. Dec. 31, 1985 = 0.

— 4637

16000 12000 8000 4000 0 -4000

S O N D J F M A M J J A

The safest trades occur when the A/D Line confirms the chart pattern for price. The chart for the DJIA and the Advance/Decline Line during 1990 show a pronounced divergence. Attempts by the A/D Line to rally were feeble and came nowhere near establishing an uptrend, except for one unsuccessful attempt in July. The divergence between highs when the Dow nudged the 3,000 level turned out to be very significant. The A/D Line is accustomed to make a top or bottom three months to a year before a major top or bottom in the overall market.

6. The number of stocks making new 52-week highs and new 52-week lows comprises an important long-term leading indicator for the underlying health of the market.

If the market is soundly based, there should be a steady stream of new highs each week. Conversely, a bear market is confirmed by a steady stream of new lows. The occurrence of a significantly lower number of new highs at successive market tops shows negative divergence that may call into question the market's ability to continue higher. The reverse holds true for bear markets. It is notable that the much higher high in the DJIA that occurred in 1990 resulted in a much smaller number of new highs than occurred at the market top in 1987.

7.   The Dow Jones Utility Index is a reliable leading indicator for the overall stock market. It is sensitive to emerging trends in interest rates and the perceptions of conservative traders. Therefore, it often turns up about three months before the overall market makes its low. Similarly, it often turns down about three months before the overall market makes its top.

8.   The definitive bible for understanding the internal dynamics of the stock market is Martin Zweig's readable book *Winning on Wall Street*. It has little relevance for Futures other than Stock Indexes but for them it is invaluable.

9.   Wellspring System entry signals occurring in conjunction with preferred lunar time periods and other major potential turning points have a particularly high chance of delivering profitable trades in Stock Index Futures.

10.   Always enter ordinary open stops when trading Stock Index Futures, in case of a huge, unexpected adverse movement. You should not use ordinary stops as the general means of closing out trades, but you cannot afford to be without disaster insurance at all times and under all circumstances when trading Index Futures. You will seldom have a good trade inadvertently stopped out if you allow about 200 to 300 points for a trade in the NYSE Composite Index and 300 to 500 points in the S&P.

11.   Finally, always remember that the stock market is subject to more emotion and erroneous opinion than almost any other market. Every cocktail party has stock market stories. However, the Wellspring System works consistently well for the stock market. Don't override its signals with ideas based on gossip and rumor.

Chapter 22

Capital Management

You might be tempted to pass this chapter, thinking that it concerns mere housekeeping.

Don't! Knowledge of how to manage your capital is as important to trading Futures successfully as knowledge of the technical indicators and knowledge of your own personality (discussed in Chapter 24).

Responsible capital management has five important elements:

1. Determining the initial size of your account;
2. Allocating capital when trading;
3. Limiting your losses;
4. Not being greedy! and
5. Pyramiding.

THE INITIAL SIZE OF YOUR ACCOUNT

Contrary to popular wisdom, you don't have to be already wealthy in order to trade Futures successfully. But, as with a retail store, you should have sufficient capital to carry enough stock to run a serious business and to withstand the contingencies that arise in any commercial venture.

The suggested optimum starting capital is $25,000 to $30,000. This amount of money permits flexibility so that you can diversify and take almost every major trading opportunity that occurs, including those in Futures requiring large initial margins.

It is possible, however, to start an account with as little as $5,000, although this amount must be regarded as a minimum. There is significantly more risk with such a small account: you can more easily be put out of business by a string of losses before starting to make money, particularly during the initial period of gaining the experience to trade successfully. There are also limitations: you would be restricted to trading only one or two small contracts at a time. But as long as you understand the risks and limitations of starting small, there is nothing wrong with doing so. Many of the biggest fortunes made from trading Futures have started as very small accounts.

One of the best ways of deciding whether you can afford to set money aside to trade Futures is to determine whether you could lose it without damaging your financial position or your peace of mind. Trading with money needed for groceries, mortgage payments or other obligations makes it almost impossible to be in the unemotional frame of mind that is required to make good trading decisions.

Regardless of how much money you start with, you should be able to get a Futures account making money consistently without losing more than $5,000 to $10,000 while learning. Therefore, if you start with an account of $25,000 to $30,000 (the optimum amount for diversification), you should budget to allow for a maximum cumulative loss of say $10,000.

As with any endeavor, you will make mistakes because of inexperience. In addition, some trades just don't work, despite good signals. But if learning on the job costs more than $10,000 in trading losses, stop trading. There must be something seriously wrong with your approach, and you should discover what it is before your losses become ruinous.

In deciding on the size of account to start with, you may find it helpful to see how and why we allocate capital to individual trades on the basis of the size of the account.

ALLOCATING TRADING CAPITAL
FOR SMALL AND START-UP ACCOUNTS

The allocation of trading capital for all accounts of $10,000 or less, and for all accounts (regardless of size) that have not banked a minimum of $10,000 in realized profits, is *three times the exchange minimum margin per contract to be traded.*

The advantage of this yardstick for allocating capital is that it allows for automatic and timely adjustment by the exchanges to accommodate variations in volatility. You need this protection as much as your broker does.

Individual brokerage houses set their own margins, which may be higher than the exchange minimums. However, they should not be substantially higher, and it should always be possible to find out from your broker what the exchange minimum margin is for any contact. (If your broker consistently requires much more than exchange minimum margins, find another one.)

Some contracts, such as certain Foods, require higher margins for nearby contracts than for the deferred. Don't be deterred from trading the nearbys because of this. Allocate three times the margin required for the deferred contracts, which should amply cover the real exposure to risk.

ALLOCATING OF TRADING CAPITAL
FOR LARGER AND ESTABLISHED ACCOUNTS

The allocation of trading capital for larger and established accounts is *two times the exchange minimum margin per contract* (compared with three times for small and start-up accounts), *provided that* the account meets all of the following qualifications:

1. a minimum of $15,000 in total available trading capital and, ideally, much more; and

2. an established record of making money, with a minimum of $10,000 in profits banked to prove it; and

3. a diversified portfolio of open positions that are trading at a profit, in at least three unrelated areas of the board, or uncommitted cash.

Note that true diversification is often much harder to achieve than you might think. For instance, a shift in sentiment about interest rates might affect not only interest rate Futures but also a wide range of Futures affected by the cost of money. The extent and duration of linkages between different Futures varies considerably over time.

ALLOWING FOR LOSSES

After a losing trade, a conservative and responsible approach to allocating capital for the next trade calls for:

1. replenishing the allocation by the amount of the loss (from your total trading capital); and/or

2. reducing the number of contracts to bring the allocation back in line.

You may be tempted to think that the Wellspring System's guidelines for allocating trading capital are unduly restrictive. However, it is a general principle of business that a well-capitalized enterprise can take advantage of opportunities when they arise, can withstand setbacks and is likely to stay in business for the long term. On the other hand, a business that constantly stretches its capital is vulnerable to a serious loss that could otherwise be absorbed as a matter of course by a well-capitalized business. In the extreme, a business stretching its capital can go under in the event of an unexpected bad loss.

Our guidelines for allocating capital steer a middle course between such conservatism that only half the available capital is ever used, and such over-exposure that the business might be endangered.

The industry's requirement when setting margins and supervising accounts is to make sure that there is enough money available to sustain a total wipe-out of the money allocated to any given trade. Our requirements are different: we need to allocate enough capital to be able to absorb several consecutive losses and still be able to come back to the market without impairing trading capital or our emotional resources.

One way of determining a reasonable allowance for maximum drawdown (maximum cumulative consecutive losses) is to test a trading system over an extended period on the basis of taking every trading signal. The Wellspring System has been tested against several markets over a six-year period to 1991. The U.S. Treasury Bond provides a representative example of this exercise.

Taking every signal delivered by the system between March 1985 and March 1991 resulted in a maximum string of four consecutive losses. These four losses, including an allowance for commissions and slippage of $150 per trade, totalled $4,475. Starting capital of three times an exchange minimum margin of $2,500, or a total of $7,500, would have left you with $3,025 for the fifth trade. If the exchange minimum margin were $3,000 (the exchanges alter margins to adjust for changes in volatility), an allocation of $9,000 to the first trade would have left $4,525 for the fifth one.

This exercise for one representative market suggests that you could make an initial allocation of capital and then continue trading the same number of contracts without replenishing your allocation when there are losses. The reality is different, however, for several reasons.

First, although there is a statistical probability of about 80% that the fifth trade will make money, this still leaves one chance in five that it too will lose money. Second, we know that after as few as one or two losses, some people lose their objectivity when making trading decisions: they either lapse into an ultra-cautious mindset that is counter-productive or into a reckless mindset that reduces trading to gambling.

The third reason is Murphy's Law of Futures Trading (which works in all businesses in its own way). This law operates to make sure that a major disaster is most apt to occur when you can least afford it. You can least afford a disaster after a string of losses has eroded your trading capital or when you take on more contracts than usual because a trade looks particularly promising. Although the T-Bond record did not include any single major loss, big ones can — and do — strike virtually everyone at some time. In Bonds, for example, you could sustain a single disaster of $4,000 or more as a result of an unforeseen earth-shaking event.

Consequently, the allocation for each trade of three times the exchange minimum margin for smaller accounts, or two times for larger and established accounts, is businesslike and not excessive.

LIMITING YOUR LOSSES

Managing losses is an inseparable component of capital management. In the extreme — which has happened to many thousands of traders — losses can wipe out trading capital to the point where there is no more left to manage.

The essential principles regarding stops and the liquidation of trades (described in Chapter 13) are therefore worth reiterating:

1. It is as important to limit your losses as it is to make profits.

2. If you are unable or unwilling to use stops, you should not be trading Futures.

3. You cannot expect to maximize your profits or minimize your losses unless you liquidate trades in accordance with the procedures for liquidating trades described in Chapter 13, regardless of whether they are showing a profit or a loss.

If you have to wrestle psychologically with taking a loss, remind yourself that taking losses in accordance with the rules is an exercise in conserving capital. Then your account will live to trade when a new opportunity arises with a majority of favorable indicators.

NOT BEING GREEDY

The rewards for allocating capital responsibly are illustrated by the following example, in which every signal delivered by the Wellspring System for T-Bonds between March 1985 and March 1991 was taken.

Profitable Trades	33 (70%)	109.15 Points	$109,469
Losing Trades	14 (30%)	(13.02)	(13,062)
Total Trades	47 (100%)	96.13 Points	$96,407
	Less allowance for commissions and slippage ($150 per trade)		7,050
	Net Profit		$89,357

This result is based on trading one contract per trade (no pyramiding). With an allocation of $7,500 in trading capital, the return on investment, after all commissions and an allowance for slippage, is 1,191%!

The mathematics of not being greedy can work spectacularly if you allocate capital responsibly and then add more contracts for subsequent trades as more money becomes available from realized profits. In the case of the Bonds, for example, taking each trade during the five-year period with as many contracts as there were multiples of $7,500, and allowing for multiple losses as well as multiple gains, resulted in a net profit of over $16 million!

While this result may seem hard to believe, there have been enough people who have achieved such returns to know that it can be done.

The point of this illustration is not to suggest that you should personally expect to make such phenomenal returns yourself, but to emphasize the potential rewards from budgeting for the worst so that you can always stay in business.

PYRAMIDING

The example of the Treasury Bonds assumed that trading capital was allocated at the start of each trade and the number of contracts remained the same while the trade was in progress. Pyramiding normally refers to adding more contracts to a position while it is under way, using unrealized profits to finance additional margin money.

Opinions about pyramiding vary widely. Some say that you should never do it. Others say that you must do it in order to capitalize to the maximum on your really good trades and to make up for your inevitable losers.

Our view is that you should generally decide on the number of contracts that you can afford to trade when you first enter the market and not add more during the course of the trade. The Wellspring System gets you in and out of the market often enough under normal circumstances so that you can review each new trade unemotionally while you are out of the market and considering the next entry.

Circumstances when we might look to pyramid additional contracts during the course of a trade could include a very rapidly moving market. It could also include a market having very small cyclical retracements so that a trade may last for many weeks or even months without a signal to liquidate.

The problem with pyramids is that a very high percentage of them result in traders making huge profits on paper, for a time, while ending with little or no profit when a sudden retracement occurs. Worse, they can sometimes swing from huge paper profits to losses that more than wipe out the entire account.

With these major reservations, there can be a place for pyramiding during the course of a trade. Here are our rules for pyramiding:

Rule 1

Start with your normal allocation of capital and your corresponding regular number of contracts, regardless of how good the prospects for a trade seem to be.

Rule 2

Add contracts only when:

a) there is a very clearly established trend; and
b) a new trading formation is completed; and
c) entry is qualified by the entry rules.

Rule 3

Never add to a losing position.

This is what the industry calls scale-down buying or scale-up selling. It is a recipe for disaster and the most common cause of staggering losses. Even if you are right in the end, time and money can easily run out first. Even limited additions to losing positions can intensify an emotional bond with a trade, thereby clouding judgment and diverting attention from other promising opportunities.

Rule 4

Never allocate more margin money to add to a pyramid. Use only the paper profit made on a trade from contracts entered earlier.

The only exception to this rule might be if you took only a partial position to start with. Then you might bring the position up to your normal weighting.

Rule 5

When adding to a position, each contract, old or new, should have available no less than twice the exchange minimum margin.

The object of the exercise is to bank profits when the trade finally turns against you, not to see how many contracts you can pile up.

Rule 6

If in doubt, don't do it!

CONCLUSION

Most of our approaches to capital management can be compared with the kind of responsible approaches necessary for managing capital in other lines of business. The nature of any business is that you must have plans and budgets, with appropriate allowances for contingencies. The seductiveness of opportunities to make a lot of money quickly must not undermine sound business practice. That the opportunities exist shows that it is a good line of business, not that it is a business that can be approached without discipline.

Chapter 23

You And Your Broker

Rule 1: Don't listen to people who stand to profit if you follow their advice. That goes for bankers, brokers and the like. [1]

This rule may seem harsh. After all, many people have an image of a broker as a trustworthy professional who personifies the statement attributed to J. P. Morgan, Jr., "The client's belief in the integrity of our advice is our best possession."

At many brokerage houses, however, the client's problems begin with the advice. Following the research department's recommendations is not likely to lead to making money, on balance.

You have seen from the discussion of market sentiment in Chapter 20 how the majority of advisers, many of whom work for brokers, are so reliably wrong at important highs and lows that you should look to do the opposite of what they recommend. In case you have any doubts about whether you should do your own homework or trust an adviser — any adviser, whether employed by a brokerage house or an independent — there is one cardinal rule: ask for the track record. If you want to be sure that the record is accurate and the advice reliable, keep track of the recommendations on paper for some time before following them with your money.

Even if the track record looks good, examine it closely to see whether its frequency of trading, average profits, average losses, proportion of commissions to net profits and overall approaches are compatible with your objectives.

The chief executive officer of an international full-service brokerage house once told the author that he knew he had a problem with the recommendations made by his Futures research department. However, he didn't propose to do anything about it because he believed that the firm's clients wouldn't follow the recommendations, however good they were. He thought that the majority of them treated Futures like gambling in Las Vegas. Therefore, all that his firm proposed to do was to provide the service. "You can't stop people from banging their brains out if they insist on doing it . . . "

---

[1] *How to Start Investing with Just $1,000*, Hume Publishing Co. Ltd., Toronto, n.d.

But this CEO was most concerned that his brokers work with renewed vigor at generating more commission revenue!

This brings us to the problem that the broker has, of being caught between the requirements of the client, the firm and himself.

THE CONFLICT OF INTEREST

Imagine a broker's office at the start of the day. The first thing that branch managers and brokers do is to check the printout for the previous day's commission run. High commissions are good, low commissions bad. If very bad, something will have to be done to "correct" the situation. This means generating more commissions quickly.

The broker's need to generate commissions can be implemented all too readily with Futures clients. The majority of them are hopelessly vulnerable. They are lured by dreams of riches, driven by greed, fear and insecurity, and seldom guided by knowledge or a trading plan. They also believe that there is a relationship between trading frequently and making money. Thus, all that the broker has to do with many clients is to make a call suggesting a trade.

Since commissions are paid only when trades are liquidated, the pressure to persuade a client to cover a position begins as soon as the trade is entered: what the broker can cash in today may lead to another trade to cash in tomorrow. The easiest trades to persuade a client to liquidate are those showing a profit. "Take your profit while it's there!" is a saying that rolls glibly off the tongue. Or, "No one ever went broke taking a profit!"

We know a better saying, "No one ever went broke taking a loss — when it's manageable!" We know that you have to get out of losing trades and let the winners run. But many, many Futures accounts contain only losing positions, while all the profits, such as they are, are taken so quickly that they never amount to anything worth having, let alone cover the losses.

Don't forget that clients want to make money. That's why they are vulnerable to being told that they should liquidate profitable positions. On the other hand, both the broker and the client are likely to be reluctant to admit to being wrong when the need arises to take a loss.

The pressure to trade frequently is a bigger bonanza for the brokerage industry than you might imagine. A rule of thumb is that annual commissions are expected to equal the combined trading equity of all Futures accounts. There is also another rule of thumb that it takes about a year, on average, for clients to lose their entire trading equity, including additions during the year.

While these numbers could hardly look more bleak, you should not be personally discouraged. All they mean is that there is a massive amount of money available to be made. As mentioned in Chapter 1, the 80/20 rule — 80 losers to 20 winners — applies with a vengeance to Futures trading. You should expect to be among the traders who make all the money lost by the rest.

In order to find profitable trades and, even more important, to let them run to a decent profit, there is unlikely to be any substitute for doing your own homework (or following an advisory service with a proven track record). There is almost certainly no point in relying on your broker's research department and still less on the broker himself. That's like asking a policeman for legal advice. The broker is not an analyst but a salesman — which is what they're called by floor brokers at the exchanges.

You still have to have a broker, though.

WHAT YOU NEED FROM A BROKER

Here is what you need:

1. Efficient and timely execution of trades and reporting of fills.
2. Accurate and understandable accounting.
3. Exchange minimum margins (or, at least, margins roughly in line with exchange minimums).
4. Price quotations when considering trades during the day and minimal factual information about forthcoming reports, etc.
5. A reasonable cost of doing business.

All of these requirements should be available from all brokers, but there are marked differences among them. Essentially, the industry is divided between full-service retail brokerage houses, which usually also deal in stocks and bonds, and Futures specialists.

The full-service firms usually charge much more for commissions, often as much as $80 to $100 per contract, compared with $20 to $40 for Futures specialists. More than half of what you pay at most full-service brokers is for advice that you don't need and for hefty commission-based paychecks for the broker, who gets 30 to 50% of the commission. As well, most full-service firms have huge overhead expenses that have nothing to do with the cost of processing your orders.

Most Futures specialists run lean and efficient businesses. Generally, the people on the phone are order-takers who are paid a salary. Most of them don't want to talk about markets and some refuse to do so. This is exactly what you need! You get all the services you need at a good price without receiving unsolicited and potentially lethal advice.

If you want a lot of price quotations, or information about reports or about the mechanics of trading, you should realize that a broker has a cost of doing business of at least $2 per minute. That has to be built into commissions one way or another.

There may be reasons such as convenience, the cost of long-distance telephone calls or the availability of quotation equipment for clients that could lead you to do business with a full-service broker. In this case, you may still be able to strike a deal on price. Most full-service brokers have some latitude for lowering commissions for clients trading a greater number of contracts and requiring less hand-holding.

BE BUSINESSLIKE

The satisfactory operation of your business requires that you have a businesslike relationship with your broker — one that engenders mutual trust and respect. For such a relationship to develop, you must be completely professional about two areas in particular: money and giving trading orders.

You should not expect to pay any more money into the account after you first open it. Thereafter, profits should look after all your needs for margin money and reserve trading capital. But in the event that you do have a margin call, you must meet it at once. And don't even think about putting on a trade before the necessary funds, in line with the requirements described in Chapter 22, are in the account. To do so would mean trading with the broker's money or, at least, with his commitment. That is completely unprofessional and unacceptable.

BE EFFICIENT WITH ORDERS

One of the most annoying things for a broker is a client who is sloppy about giving orders. Not only is it time consuming and inefficient, but it can lead to errors and arguments that may take a lot of time and money to sort out.

An overly familiar or sloppy relationship can result in an order being placed along the lines of, "Oh, George, I want to sell my Cattle, please."

George cannot be expected to know whether you are dealing in Live Cattle or Feeders, which month you are in, how many contracts you have and whether you are long or short the market.

Efficient communication goes something like this:

"I have an order, please."

"Ready."

"Account Number 12345. Sell five December Live Cattle market."

"Account Number 12345. Sell five December Live Cattle market."

With the precision of a pilot talking to an air traffic controller, the minimum of words are exchanged, and the precise order is read back word for word by the broker.

KEEP RECORDS

To be efficient about running your business, you must keep a diary of your trading activity.

Before actually placing an order, write it in the diary so that you can insure its accuracy by reading it off to the broker. Then mark down the time of giving the order and the most recent price. Since it should take no more than two minutes to have your order filled, this information will permit you to check whether you got a reasonable fill.

In the event of a disagreement about the price of a fill, you can have the broker get a printout from the exchange which will show the prices at which business was transacted when your order was filled. Each party along the line of communication accepts personal responsibility for handling orders correctly. On the rare occasions when a mistake occurs, don't be shy, within reason, about having a fill price adjusted if you didn't get what you should have.

It is popularly thought that some brokers get their clients better fills than other brokers are able to get. For all practical purposes, this isn't true. In any actively traded market you can safely place a market order and have it filled at the current price. Only when a market is moving fast are there likely to be surprises, good or bad, but you can still count on being treated honestly.

Besides the details of each trade, your diary should contain details of all outstanding open orders (usually stops). These should be marked with a highlighter so that you can see at once what open orders are outstanding.

Make a regular practice of checking your open orders with the broker every week or two, depending on how actively you are trading. This should be done outside market hours. If in doubt, take the time to check with the broker because no one wants the trouble of fixing up an unintended trade.

FINAL WORD ON BROKERS

If you want to trade Futures, you have to have a broker — just as you have to have a dentist if you want to look after your teeth. By and large, your dentist is unlikely to drill for imaginary cavities. But the brokerage industry is subject to far more insidious pressures to generate business than you might ever have thought possible. Your Futures broker is all too likely, often despite the best of intentions, to be a party to creating an enormous cavity in your Futures account — if you let it happen.

It is hoped that this book may help some brokers see the potential for developing a sound and growing long-term business, based on their clients making money. But don't count on finding such a person to be your own broker. In fact, don't even bother to try to find one. This is your business and you are responsible for it.

Be nice to your broker if he is an efficient order-taker and fill-reporter. But don't ever talk about markets!

* * * * *

The following books are strongly recommended for their readability and for background information on how the industry operates:

Lies Your Broker Tells You, Thomas D. Saler, Walker, 1989.

The Wall Street Gurus: How You Can Profit From Investment Newsletters, Peter Brimelow, Key Porter, 1986.

Chapter 24

The Winning Attitude

For a winning attitude, the will to win counts as nothing: everyone claims a will to win. What counts is the will *to prepare* to win. That's what makes the difference between wanting to win and actually doing so.

PREPARING TO WIN

One way of testing your own will to be a successful Futures trader is to ask yourself some practical questions:

Am I prepared to learn the business by thoroughly learning the system?
Am I prepared to follow the system's signals when I see them as readily as I respond to traffic lights when driving a car?
Will I really use the capital management guidelines, or will I cheat and expose the business to greater risk?
Will I do the required homework every day for markets that I am trading or thinking of trading?

Few people could be expected to give an unhedged answer to all these questions. However, your success is likely to be in proportion to your readiness to do the work required to be successful.

A further way of preparing yourself to be successful is to consider the psychological weaknesses to which you may be susceptible, so that you can consciously guard against them. Here are the seven deadly sins of Futures trading.

1. Impatience

Impatience is the first deadly sin, afflicting virtually all traders at least sometimes. Traders often set themselves up like runners at the starting blocks. A big trade looks to be shaping up and it is all too tempting to jump the starting gun, possibly several times, instead of waiting for the indicators to fall into place that suggest the trade is ready to start.

Similarly, traders can be so impatient to take profits that they drop out well before the trade has run its course. Impatience leading to taking profits prematurely may mean that there are never any of the big profits that make trading really worthwhile.

This book has discussed, among other things, consolidations and trading ranges, surges and retracements, cycles and landmarks in time. All of these recurring elements of price fluctuation can take a surprisingly long time to work themselves out. In a sense, they are tests of your patience which will invariably trap the impatient. Constantly remind yourself of this fact.

Another way to deal with impatience is to review old charts to remind yourself of just how long good trades can take to unfold. For example, the weekly D-Mark chart on page 65 indicates that each of the major bull and bear moves lasted for several years. The weekly Copper chart on page 85 shows almost three years of trading range action before the big bull market suddenly started in 1987. And remember: waiting patiently for such trades and then trading them patiently is the only way to make a fortune from trading Futures.

2. Fear

Many traders are afraid to take the strongest signals, the ones that may have moved powerfully before entry, and often lead to the biggest and best trades. Many traders are also afraid to take a loss, particularly when it is large.

You may be able to identify powerful signals, which you know from past experience have an excellent probability of making a substantial profit. But you can't bring yourself to place the order. So you stay out of the market altogether or take another trade with a very weak signal or, worst of all, take the strong trade well after it has gone on its way.

The remedy for fear under these circumstances lies in determining why fear assails you. Do you really believe the signals? If you don't, continue checking out the system until you know in your bones that it works. As well, realize that many traders have to learn to take such trades, just as a diver has to learn to dive off the top board or an airline pilot has to learn to believe his instruments. Successful traders overcome their fear by entering these trades with just one contract until they build enough confidence to enter the number of contracts that they are accustomed to trade.

If you're afraid to take a loss, you have probably failed to follow the rules for placing stops or for liquidating trades. As with the fear of taking strong entry signals, one remedy is to trade on paper until the evidence convinces you that the rules for stops and liquidation of trades really do work.

Also, face the fact that if you don't use stops, are afraid to use stops or if you ever cancel stops and leave a trade without one, you should not be trading Futures. Unlike many traders, you can't excuse yourself by saying that you were uncertain where a stop should be. It is always clear from the Chapter 13 rules where a stop should be placed.

3. Greed

Many traders enter more contracts than their financial resources can support if the trade goes wrong. As well, many traders can't liquidate a trade when a profit turns to a loss.

Traders sometimes see a trade that looks like such a winner that they cannot resist entering more, often many more, than their regular number of contracts. If this is your style, think of Joe Granville's words of caution, "If it's obvious, it's obviously wrong!" Remember, too, that Murphy's Law of Futures Trading always lies in wait for the greedy.

Once a trade starts moving strongly in the desired direction, some traders start to see thousand dollar bills. Consequently, they often decide to bank a profit immediately rather than wait for a signal to liquidate. These traders rarely bank major profits and some of them never bank enough to cover their losses. Other traders stay in a trade too long, trying to recapture the profit that once was there, rather than accept that the market has no intention of accommodating them. These traders often see profits turn to a loss because they initially fail to enter a stop in the right place or ignore a signal to liquidate. Then they refuse to recognize repeated signals confirming that the market is no longer going in the direction of their trade.

For these traders, greed outweighs fear. But, as with fear, one remedy is to examine *what you tell yourself* about a trade when it contradicts what the system tells you about it.

4. Hope

Traders turn to hope when they have no technical reason to be in a trade. Hope is an abdication of control to the market and it very seldom works. It is easier to wait for tomorrow than to make a decision today. But that can be ruinously costly.

If you ever start hoping for a trade, stop hoping and get out.

Believing in luck and clinging to hope are emotionally related. Both imply reliance on external forces rather than taking personal responsibility for one's life and trading.

To some traders, a belief in luck is central to their view of how to trade Futures successfully and, even more important, how to explain away bad trades: they were unlucky. These traders, often unconsciously, invoke luck and ignore signals. A trader on the wrong side of the Wheat market, for example, might say, "With any luck it will rain on the weekend . . . ," rather than act on a signal to get out of the market.

It is true that all traders have good and bad luck from time to time. But good luck in Futures trading, as in life generally, tends to happen to those who are already doing the right things to be successful. Bad luck tends to strike those who ignore valid signals, take inordinate risk or don't do their homework.

5. Pride

Pride assails traders who believe that their own personal power or knowledge is superior to markets or trading systems.

Many otherwise extremely successful people bring to Futures trading the attitude of the conquering hero. Successful experience in wrestling with business problems may lead to the conclusion, for example, that Gold is the only store of value worth considering or, contrariwise, that it should be worth nothing. But the power of the mind over markets is no contest when there is a conflict: markets always win.

Proud traders who cannot accept the superiority of markets often rationalize losing positions. Typically these traders will say, "I'm showing a loss but it doesn't matter. I'm in the trade for the long term." Or they will say, "I've moved my stop out further because I know the market's going to turn." Many traders who have told themselves that they are taking the long-term view end up with losses in the order of $8,000 on a single Lumber contract, $5,000 on one Sugar, $15,000 on one Gold — or no account at all. Markets can make the long term all too short when it comes to humbling those who trade on pride, rather than on following the rules.

6. Carelessness

After a very big profit or a very big loss, depending on your personality, it is easy to get sloppy about doing your homework. Therefore, monitor your actions and your emotions after a big gain or a big loss. If you find it difficult to approach the business methodically and unemotionally after such a period, take a break from trading. It is not necessary to trade every day or to take every trade that comes along.

7. Gambling

Many people are drawn to Futures trading because they see it as similar to taking a trip to Atlantic City or Las Vegas. These are the people who maintain the myth that you must be a gambler or a high roller in order to be a successful Futures trader.

But gambling, by definition, involves trusting to chance rather than taking planned and calculated risks. Every trader will occasionally misread signals but that is not the same as trading without doing your homework. That is — don't delude yourself — gambling.

Some people either cannot, or will not, stop gambling and Futures offers them a venue for doing it. If you recognize that you are a member of this group, you should, at the least, consider another form of gambling, where you are likely to lose less than in Futures.

TIPS FOR MAKING TRADING EASIER

Watching for emotional pitfalls is one aspect of the psychology of Futures trading. But it is equally important to bring to trading an attitude that it should be psychologically rewarding and fun, as well as profitable.

174

Don't be deterred from thinking positively about Futures trading as a business because of preconceived ideas about risk. There is nothing inherently more risky or more of a gamble in running a Futures trading business than there is in running a factory or a convenience store. In fact, there are similarities between a Futures trading business and an insurance company: both require the allocation of capital systematically and in the knowledge that both profits and losses have to be budgeted for as a matter of course.

Any business is risky if approached without knowledge and planning. Futures trading is no exception. However, it has certain major advantages over other businesses when approached with knowledge, planning and discipline: you are your own boss and don't have to worry about customers or employees. And the potential rewards qualify Futures trading as one of the most exceptional business opportunities of this age. Or any age.

One of the keys to successful trading is to reward yourself with the fruits of success. While Futures trading is more immediately involved in making money than most other businesses, making money should have a purpose. After a good trade, give yourself an extra pay check. Go out to dinner. Take a vacation. Or do whatever you dreamed might become possible from successful Futures trading.

Another way to maintain your emotional balance is to repay your starting capital. You will find that it becomes easier to trade when you are working with money that you made in the market. That relieves the stress of relating money that you put at risk to the work and saving required to get started. It is also an exercise in good management to be the owner of a business with a zero cost base. Then, if the worst came to the very worst, you would be able to start again if you had to.

Also, make a point of liquidating any losing trades in your account at the same time as you liquidate a profitable trade. It is all too easy to bank profitable trades while retaining losers. This is the opposite of what is required to make money in the long run.

This book cannot cover the psychological aspects of Futures trading as comprehensively as the technical aspects. The following books are particularly recommended for further exploration in this area. They also contain good bibliographies.

Games Investors Play, Michael Chisholm, Butterfly & Buttercups, Bloomery Star Route, Winchester, VA 22601, 1984.

Investor's Quotient: The Psychology of Successful Investing in Commodities and Stocks, Jacob Bernstein, John Wiley, 1990.

Overcoming the Fear of Success, Martha Friedman, Seaview Books, 1980.

The Luck Factor: Why Some People Are Luckier Than Others And How You Can Become One Of Them, Max Gunter, Macmillan, 1977.

Chapter 25

Putting It All Together

This book has shown you, step by step, what you need to know to set up a Futures trading business that should make you a fortune within five years. But you have to bring it all together to make it happen. Step by step.

There's no substitute for approaching the business methodically and in this sequence:

1. Learn the system.

    It must become second nature to you, like driving a car, to read the indicators. You don't have to carry every detail in your head. But you must know the general principles thoroughly. And you must know where to find the details when a question arises for which you don't have the immediate answer.

2. Set up the business with all of the supplies described in Chapter 2.

    Don't cut corners. You may work the business only part-time. That, in fact, is all that you should ever do, since trading just doesn't take all day every day. But you do have to set it up as a real business.

3. Prove the system for yourself with paper-trading.

    Repeated practice with different contracts should give you the knowledge and the confidence that you need to put real money into actual trades.

4. Don't open an account with money that you can't afford to lose if the worst befalls you: a minimum of $5,000; better $10,000; optimum $25-30,000.

    It is essential that you be able to replace your initial trading capital from other sources in case it turns out that you personally can't get a Futures account to make money.

The risk of not getting the account off the ground is much less if you start with a larger account that has the flexibility to diversify. It's like trying to start a retail store: you have to have enough stock to run the business. Your defense against losing more than you are willing to is to set a limit on losses, say $5,000 or $10,000 at the most. If you reach this limit, stop trading to analyze what is going wrong.

5. Be patient about waiting for indicators to fall into place to signal superior trades. And recognize that this can take weeks or months to happen.

It's a truism that timing is everything. That is what the Wellspring System is all about — like surfing and catching the wave as it crests. Given that you can make a great deal of money when you get a big trade right, there is no point in being impatient and dissipating your trading capital by taking second-rate trades that automatically increase the probability of a loss. It pays to be patient.

Some successful traders make only a dozen or so trades each year, but they are big winners. It doesn't matter if you leave money sitting in your account until the maximum number of indicators come together for a big trade. That may annoy your broker but it's your business, not his. Better to have the money there when a good opportunity arises than to fritter it away on trades having substandard potential.

6. Each day keep an eye on the *weekly* charts. They are the key for knowing which markets to trade, which to avoid and when to stop working a market that you are currently trading.

7. Take your losses exactly when the system says to get out, whether by stop or by order to liquidate.

You don't have to be a great trader to be successful as long as you get out of your losing trades when you are supposed to.

8. Review the Wellspring System in its entirety at least once a month.

It's surprising how important details can escape you.

9. Review your trading record at the end of each month to examine what went right and why. But it's even more important to determine what went wrong in order not to repeat your mistakes.

IDENTIFYING POTENTIAL MARKETS TO TRADE

Three kinds of indicators are used to identify potential markets to trade: weekly chart indicators, daily chart indicators and indicators that are not related directly to charts. The checklist on the next page should be used initially to identify potential markets to trade, using the weekly and non-chart indicators.

If a majority of these indicators confirm a market to trade and if the non-confirming indicators do not, on balance, negate the ones that are favorable, use the daily chart indicators on the checklist to validate entry to the market. A trading formation on the daily chart and the entry rules serve as the final confirmation to place an order.

In going through the checklist, it is important to note that the trading formations having the highest probability of success are those that occur:

a) at expected cyclical lows when the RSI and stochastics have begun to turn up from a low level (when buying) or at expected tops when the RSI and stochastics have begun to decline from a high level (when selling);

b) on a breakout through support or resistance, or through a trendline or channel line; and

c) during the course of a strongly trending and rapidly moving market, when the trend continuation trading formation, described on page 22, frequently occurs.

Support and resistance levels, trendlines and channel lines can create some of the most seductive traps that exist in all Futures trading. Chapters 10, 11 and 12 describe how price frequently turns back at these points. Trading formations completed just prior to penetration of these levels may be a trap. The probability of a successful trade is thus increased substantially by waiting for a breakout to occur. When the breakout occurs with a gap opening, it is often highly profitable to enter right away rather than wait until the close. In any case, there should be a strong surge through the relevant level and a close in the top or bottom 25% of the day's range (depending on whether you are buying or selling). A market that merely pokes its nose through one of these lines may well have the same result as one that fails to go through at all — a sudden surge in the opposite direction, after looking to see whether there was any follow-through to the breakout and finding none.

THE RATIO OF WINNING TRADES TO LOSING TRADES

The importance of bringing together coincident indicators is dramatically illustrated by seeing what happens to net profits when the proportion of losing trades is reduced.

Chapter 8 showed how closing price reversals on a sample weekly chart had a 55% probability of delivering a profitable signal, while closing price reversals that coincided with an established trend or an emerging trend had a 64% probability of delivering a profitable signal.

Checklist for Identifying Markets to Trade and for Entering Trades

Contract_____ Price_____ Buy_____ Sell_____ Date _____

Weekly Chart Indicators
1. Are prices near historic/10-year highs?_____ Historic/10-year lows? _____
2. How is the market defined? Bull_____ Bear_____ Erratic_____
3. Is there an emerging W-Formation?_____ M-Formation_____
4. Is there a trading range?_____ Other pattern _____
5. Which trading formation(s)? _____
6. Where is price vs. trendlines?_____ Channel lines _____
7. Where is price vs. support?_____ Resistance _____
8. What is cyclical timing? Long-term_____ Intermediate _____
9. What are possible target levels? _____
10. What are negating indicators? _____
11. Do weekly chart indicators support the trade? _____

Non-Chart Indicators
1. Any important fundamental information? _____
2. Is the market normal?_____ Inverted _____
3. Market sentiment: Current level_____ Trend _____
4. CoT/Large speculators: Net_____ Change _____ Trend _____
5. Vol./O.I.: Recent action_____Relation to 5-year average _____

Daily Chart Indicators
1. Where is price vs. trendlines?_____ Channel lines _____
2. Where is price vs. support?_____Resistance _____
3. What is cyclical timing? Monthly: Day_____ Other _____
4. Where are landmarks in time? _____RSI_____ Stochastics _____
5. What is initial target price?_____ Further targets _____
6. Is there a gap?_____ Island_____ 5 Consecutive Closes _____
7. Which trading formation(s)? _____
8. Is this strongest/weakest market in group?_____ In delivery month? _____
9. What are negating indicators? _____
10. Is this a first-class trade? _____

Capital Management
Total equity_____ Available equity_____ Exchange margin _____
Budget margin_____ No. of contracts_____ Budget as % of total equity _____
Expected entry price_____ Stop price_____ Loss if stopped out _____

Entry
Trade entered_____ Contracts_____ Initial Protective Stop _____
Stop changes _____

Exit Price_____ Profit/loss per contract_____ Total net _____

Comments: _____
_____

Consider the mathematics of improving the overall results of your trading by using these two indicators together rather than separately. For the purpose of illustration, we assume an increase in profitable signals from 50% to 75%. Used separately, 100 trades would deliver 50 profits and 50 losses. Used together, we expect 75 profits and 25 losses.

A reasonable assumption (based on Appendix II) for average profits and losses per trade might be $1,000 and $500 respectively. A ratio of 50% profitable trades to losing trades would deliver $50,000 in profits and $25,000 in losses. A ratio of 75% profitable trades to losing trades would deliver $75,000 in profits versus $12,500 in losses.

The result is a ratio of profits to losses of six to one. While this may seem high, and possibly unachievable in the long run, your paper-trading should lead you to *believe* that a ratio of at least three to one is possible to achieve consistently.

If you truly believe in yourself and the system, it will be easier to plan specifically to reduce your proportion of losing trades. This is done by trading only when a majority of coincident indicators confirm a trade and when trades signaled in conjunction with important negating indicators are avoided.

LET THE MARKETS DO THE WORK

It is an essential component of running the business that you relax. The Wellspring System has been developed for the purposes of making money from bigger trades and of avoiding stress.

Leave the stress to the day traders who sit in front of a quotation machine all day. You are far more likely to make money by not standing over your trades and fretting, provided that you are absolutely diligent about doing your homework each day and following the system. You may find that you trade only once a month in a market that you have identified as qualified for trading. And you may hold on to a good trade for several weeks or even months. But by trading infrequently, and only when the signals are really good, you are likely to make far more money than is made by people who constantly watch the markets and trade often.

LOSSES

One area where action and vigilance are particularly required is in getting out of markets to cut losses. Up to a point you can let stops do the work, particularly with newly entered positions. But there is no substitute for action when there are clear signals to liquidate a trade.

If this point has been labored throughout this book, it is because it is the aspect with which all traders have some difficulty and with which many traders have a lot of difficulty. Taking losses becomes much easier once you have banked good profits and when you don't need any particular trade to make money. Everyone or almost everyone, excepting only the truly committed losers, wants to make money rather than lose it. This means that you have to think positively about getting rid of losing trades. Think of them as you would think of getting rid of a toothache. And don't fuss over them once they're gone. Then you can get on with thinking positively about your winners and about new opportunities. Getting out of a bad trade frees up both financial and emotional capital to move on with running the business.

Ed Seykota, a professional trader with an excellent record, is quoted (*Forbes*, September 4, 1989) as saying that the elements of successful trading are, "one, cutting losses, two, cutting losses and three, cutting losses . . ."

Van K. Tharp, in the article reprinted in Appendix I, quotes Jack Schwager:

> Another frequent theme [of successful traders]was the emphasis on the idea that losing is part of the game. If you can't accept losses or take them easily, you can't be an efficient trader. Most readers might think this means only taking your losses quickly so that small losses do not turn into account-destroying loses. While this is true, accepting that losses are part of the game also means that fear of losing does not prevent a trader from putting on a potentially profitable position, or cause a trader to get out of a position that is good too quickly. *A loss that follows the game plan is not a bad trade, it is part of the game plan.* [Emphasis added.]

Although both Seykota and Schwager stress the need to cut losses, in practical terms it is essential to have parameters for knowing when to take this action. The Wellspring System tells you precisely when to cut losses, as well as when to get out of profitable trades. Consequently, if you are not making money, the reason is almost certainly that you are not following the system.

WHICH CONTRACT TO TRADE

You should normally trade in the nearest contract that has at least a month to run before the first notice day, unless there are special considerations relating to premiums and discounts (as discussed in Chapter 15). When a trade lasts longer than a month, you can always roll the position forward. What you lose in commissions, you will normally more than make up in increased profit resulting from greater favorable movement in the nearby contract. Also, because the deferred months in some markets are relatively illiquid, you may get better fills by trading the nearer contract months.

Only trade a deferred month when there is a pronounced difference in the strength of different expiry months. Then buy the strongest month or sell the weakest.

The same principle applies when you are faced with a choice between trading two commodities in the same general area of the board. If Corn is stronger than Soybeans, buy Corn. If the Swiss Franc is weaker than the D-Mark, sell the Swiss. It's a loser's psychology to think that you can take from the strong and give to the weak. That may be good politics, but it's lousy Futures trading. Go with the flow!

STAY WITH GOOD TRADES

Once you find a strongly trending market, keep working it until it is mined out. If you are stopped out or get out for a retracement, wait for the next trading formation and go right back in. Trading markets is a bit like riding a bucking bronco. Markets will do crazy things, kick you about and bite, and sometimes buck you off. But if you have a clearly trending market, the chances are good that it will keep on going — possibly much farther than you might have thought possible.

FINAL WORD

You can never know all that there is to know about trading Futures, any more than you can about any business. But you don't have to know everything, or even try to. The late J. Paul Getty, the famous oilman reputed to have been the richest man in the world, said that you have to be right in business only 50% of the time to be successful. That is enough to be successful in Futures trading also, although you are likely to do better. *The important thing is to run it as a business.*

You may be brilliant at running the business or only middling. But with this book there is little doubt that even middling success should be very substantial in the long run.

And if things get you down, remember this saying: "Good judgment comes from experience. Experience comes from bad judgment!"

The most stressful demands of judgment have now been relieved for you, but you cannot relax your own discipline. So, with that final admonition . . .

Best wishes and good trading!

* * *

This book was written in order to work out and to put in writing a reliable trading system for personal use and for generating trading signals for a Futures advisory service. If you wish to see how someone else puts the system to use, or if you prefer to have someone else do the day-to-day work, you are invited to write to The Wellspring Futures Newsletter, P.O. Box 7243, Ottawa, Ontario, Canada, K1L 8E3. In any case, all comments and suggestions will be appreciated.

C. A.

APPENDIX I

Wizards: Minds Over Markets
by Van K. Tharp

Jack Schwager, commodity trader and confessed system skeptic, has been a familiar name in commodity trading for a number of years. His 1984 book, *A Complete Guide to the Futures Market*, laid out most tested techniques along with other methodologies.

His latest book, *The Market Wizards: Interviews with Top Traders* (Simon & Schuster, New York) might be considered a companion to his technical tools book. *Wizards* brings home some of the more important, and often overlooked elements, of successful trading — not magical systems, but the beliefs that have made the most successful traders what they are today. Appropriately, trading psychologist Van K. Tharp interviewed Schwager while he was in the process of writing *Wizards*. What follows is a distillation of their six-hour discussion and follow-up questions. — Ed.

* * * * *

You've completed The Market Wizards. You've spent a lot of time talking with different top traders and you've had a chance to think about their responses. At this point, what do you think it takes to be a top trader?
The following are not in any particular order, just the order that I think of them. To begin, confidence in your ability to consistently win as a trader over the long run is absolutely essential. Admittedly, this is a bit of a Catch 22 proposition: in order to be a winning trader, you need to have confidence; but in order to have confidence, you need to be a winning trader. That aspect, however, does not diminish the importance of confidence. The one absolute common denominator among all the traders I interviewed was a confidence in their continued ability to win over the long run. Everything else stemmed from this confidence.

Another critical factor is discipline. While this may sound like a cliché, it is probably the single most mentioned word that cropped up when the top traders tried to explain what made them so successful.

The top traders tend to be very independent. With few exceptions, they restrict their trading decisions to their own opinions (or systems). The importance of not being swayed by the crowd was a frequently mentioned point. While this may not be very surprising, many of the traders I interviewed also stressed the importance of not being influenced even by other superior traders. This has to do with the importance of sticking with your own approach, because that is the only thing you can have confidence in. As one trader said, "If my only reason for being in a trade is because Bruce recommended it, I am not going to have the confidence to stay with that position if it starts going against me."

Superior success at trading often involves extraordinary hard work. Many traders have devoted their lives to reaching their success level. The amount of reading and analysis some of them do is staggering. For example, one trader follows and intricately analyzes economies and political events in virtually every country with a meaningfully traded currency. Another trader follows the world economy, the world currency markets, the world stock markets, futures markets and individual stocks in various countries. The same trader has also studied the history of these various markets often going back into the 19th century. Another trader has explored virtually every technical methodology under the sun and their interrelationships in stocks, options and futures. Being a great trader is hard work. There are no shortcuts.

I can think of a couple of exceptions and if there are a few exceptions, then I tend to think that element is not an essential characteristic. The people I'm thinking about tend to be traders who only trade a few times each year in each market. These traders are generally right about these moves and make outstanding rates of return. On the average, they probably only spend a couple of hours a day on market-related activity. All of those people did a lot of research and study to get where they were, but now trading, itself, is not that difficult. A second comment is that even the people who constantly put in long hours don't really consider what they do to be hard work. They do it because they love it.

Very frequently, the traders I interviewed mentioned their love for analysis, the markets and trading. They associated trading and analysis with game-like qualities. Some of the statements that came up included "(the market) is a big three-dimensional puzzle . . . Market analysis is like a tremendous multidimensional chessboard . . . (Picking a winning stock) is like a giant treasure hunt." One trader, when asked about his success, responded, "I feel my success comes from my love of the markets. There is no question that this is what I am supposed to do with my life."

I believe every person I interviewed had an overwhelming desire and persistence to succeed as a trader. In a number of cases, they wiped out more than once, but something inside of them told them to just keep at it, because eventually they would succeed. This may just be one of those factors you either have or don't have. Although winning trading may be teachable, extraordinary successful trading may not be, and this may be an example of why.

I call that commitment. Many people just do not have the commitment to be successful as traders. What else do they have in common?

The top traders have a game plan or a methodology, they don't just shoot from the hip. The existence of an effective methodology makes their high confidence level possible, which as I stated before, is a key ingredient to success.

Another frequent theme was the emphasis on the idea that losing is part of the game. If you can't accept losses or take them easily, you can't be an efficient trader. Most readers might think this means only taking your losses quickly so that small losses do not turn into account-destroying losses. While this is true, accepting that losses are part of the game also means that the fear of losing does not prevent a trader from putting on a potentially profitable position, or cause a trader to get out of a position that is good too quickly. A loss that follows the game plan is not a bad trade, it is part of the game plan. This ties in with the confidence element mentioned before. Since superior traders are extremely confident they will win, it is easy for them to accept losses as part of the process.

Patience is another critical element. A number of traders stressed the importance of waiting for the right trade to come along. A phrase that Jim Rogers used sticks in my mind, "I just wait until there is money lying in the corner and all I have to do is go over there and pick it up. I do nothing in the meantime."

What do those traders have in common, in terms of their personalities, their psychology (i.e., self-analysis), their risk control and money management, and their trading styles?

I realize something that strikes me as a bit odd. Many of the traders I interviewed could be described as quiet, introverted and soft-spoken. This is surprising when you consider that the popular image of a large, successful trader is probably more closely associated with such adjectives as flamboyant and loud. Despite their enormous financial success, the traders I interviewed did not come across as overwhelmed by their own self importance. In fact, many of them were downright modest. And I mean modest in a real sense rather than in a controlled way. For example, one trader with a remarkable win/loss ratio would say such things as, "It will be obvious when the market bottoms." He seemed to have no concept that what was obvious to him was by no means obvious to the rest of the world.

As far as risk control, in most cases it was of paramount importance, with the traders following very rigid rules or guidelines. However, surprisingly, in some cases, risk control, as we normally think of it, was not readily evident. By this, I means the trader would often take a position he felt was correct and hold it even if the market moved substantially against him. In fact, he might even add to the position in such cases. Obviously, this style of trading takes enormous confidence, accuracy and skill, not to mention courage.

How do such traders avoid catastrophic losses? I think the answer consists of two elements: diversification and extraordinary accuracy on the trades they really believe in.

In regards to trading styles, I saw no consistent patterns. Trading styles ranged from cerebral to wired.

Finally, I would note that the top traders tended to be strong-willed and inner-directed.

I noticed that the traders you interviewed had little in common in terms of methodology. Some were fundamentalists, others were technicians and others were both. Some were mechanical and others were intuitive. What conclusions can you draw form that?

That's a good point and one that I emphasized myself in the book's final wrap-up chapter. The contrast, in fact, was striking. For example, one trader commented, "I haven't met a rich technician. Excluding, of course, technicians who sell their technical services and make a lot of money." . . . Also, as you imply, some traders were 100% system followers, while others never made a single system-generated trade, in some cases, even expressing the sentiment that systems were for suckers.

Given these direct contradictions, it is obvious that as great as the individuals I interviewed were as traders, some of them were obviously wrong in their beliefs about the efficacy of different trading methods. The success of the technicians disproves the claims of the adamant fundamentalists and vice versa; the success of the system traders invalidates the skepticism of some of the pure intuitive traders. The point is that the type of method is unimportant. What is important is that the method fit the belief system and style of the individual trader. Otherwise, the trader will not be able to achieve the high degree of confidence that is apparently one of the essential elements exhibited by top traders.

I used to call one of my tasks of top trading Market Analysis. Now, I think it has little to do with market analysis. The task involves developing a low-risk idea, and you can develop low-risk ideas with a number of different methodologies. What else do they have in common?

Another lesson is psychology and discipline are apparently much more critical than the type of method or approach employed. I believe these observations also help explain why such a small percentage of people make money trading purchased systems. Even if one restricts the universe of systems to those that are profitable, most system buyers will still lose money trading these systems. Why? First, since they did not develop the system, and in the case of a black box system will not even have any idea how the system works, they're not likely to have any depth of confidence in the system. Thus, when the system goes through a losing streak as all systems inevitably will, they will be prone to abandon the system often just before it begins to make money again. Also, the odds are slim that any purchased system will closely match a given trader's intrinsic style.

If you could narrow it down to any one element, what would come closest to being the Holy Grail secret of trading success? Consider all aspects of trading here, not just methodology.

The Holy Grail is not a specific method, because the method is completely different for different top traders. The Holy Grail is a state of knowing that you have a method that gives you an edge and sticking to it. I know everyone reading this going to say, "Yes, sure, but tell me a specific method that will give me the edge." There's the rub. If it were that easy, we'd all be millionaires. All I can tell by inference from the traders I interviewed is that when you find it, you'll know. I say by inference because I have personally never arrived at that point of complete confidence. That's why I've only managed to be a profitable trader over the years, not a super trader. In other words, knowing the nature of the Holy Grail still doesn't guarantee you can find it.

Although you are by no means a super trader, you are still way above average. What do you think is important about trading? Is there anything we haven't mentioned that you think is important to your success?

Well, I recognize that trading is the only way I will be able to achieve financial independence. Secondly, trading has been my career. I have made a lot of good recommendations, but I will never consider myself successful until I make at least what I consider a small fortune. It is not for the money actually, I just want the sense of doing well.

There was a point last year to where I had done quite well and then had a terrible period of trading. I had noticed a Salvation Army guy at the local train station and I decided that if I got back to my prior peak, I would give him a small percent of every thousand dollars I made. I loved doing that. It was just this great feeling. Any time I went by I would put in a $10 or $20 bill. He thought that was a lot of money, but it wasn't. It was just doing something nice and it was a concrete connection with my doing well in trading. I felt real positive about that.

Did your trading change as a result of doing that?

My account went straight up. Virtually every week I put money in the guy's can. Which means I was making money every week, I mean virtually every week, which is pretty incredible. Actually, when I made that mental commitment, I started doing it and then I recouped everything I lost and I actually started making new highs in my account equity.

I've heard similar stories from people. It seems that giving like that changes your mental state and makes you much more receptive to making money. Incidentally, that may help you resolve the dilemma of how you can be confident before you are a winning trader. What else do you think is important in order to be successful as a trader?

Well, you have to be able to cut your losses. If you don't, sooner or later you will go back to zero. You can't be loyal to a position. In my early years I was a terrible, terrible trader. I was probably as bad a trader as you could be. I probably started off like a cripple trying to run a marathon. I have learned from experience. I have absolutely no loyalty to market position and I think that is good, that is one of the things that I do right.

I think you have to be flexible enough not only to get out, but actually reverse your position and that is something I do that is important.

One of the things that top traders do is to really put their foot on the accelerator when they have these really good trades. One trader told me, "Hey, I have two big trades a year, but those two big trades do it, and I get returns over 100% a year." When all the market indicators really line up, they heavily commit to a position and make a very large return.

You have to be organized. A lot of specifics like stops, exiting the market correctly, etc., all come under the general frame of being organized.

You have to be focused to follow a set pattern of looking at markets. I think that if you are emotionally troubled by other things, that confuses trading. If you don't focus, it blurs the position.

Something I learned a long time ago is to never trade against your basic feeling. So what I used to do, for example, I would be right in the long-term market and be so intent on a correction that I actually would get out of my long-term position and try to trade the correction. Never go against your basic feeling!

What do you think contrasts you from the average trader who just plunges into the market and loses a lot of money?

That is pretty easy. For extended periods, although I was financially comfortable, I didn't have money I felt I could trade with so I didn't trade. For me, that is like a system because I know not to trade with money I can't really afford to lose. I am really good about taking very, very small initial risks. Once you have the market's money, then you can take more risk.

I always pride myself on being flexible. I can be bullish one day and bearish the next. I thing that is real good.

I can look at charts and have some potential leverage, not to a degree that I am ever very, very confident, but enough so that I should win over the long run.

On the fundamental side, I sometimes am very good about picking a major move situation. Yet, in my case, the weakness is always coming away with a much smaller portion of the pot than I should have. At least I feel good about being able to identify the major move in those cases.

I have no problem buying a market when it is falling if I feel that it is basically a real bull market. I have to have some confidence to be able to go into a falling market and buy it or to go into a rising market and sell it. I won't just do it through a free fall. It must be under the right circumstances, a market that I believe could have a major trend in the opposite direction.

I don't do anything reckless. I am very, very conservative, so I will trade one, two, three contracts. I will never put on 20, 25 contracts at a time. I never put on any really major positions, so I don't take big risks.

When I am methodical, I have made money. I had my specific rules, I was keeping a trader's diary, so I guess anything I do which is organized and systematic is beneficial. I do an element planning and I find that I do best when I plan systematically.

Here is one thing I do and it's worked for me. I am a perfectionist in what I do. I find it easier just to do something the way I can, even if it means doing a lot of work, than trying to find something halfway. I try to do things the right way, not take the short cut.

What did you learn about trading that you didn't know prior to doing The Market Wizards?

Each person reading this book will come away with different insights that are personally relevant. What may be unimportant to one reader may be absolutely critical to another. But not to dodge the question, some of the personal insights I experienced:

- Discipline is much more than a cliché.
- Patience waiting for the right trade is absolutely critical.
- To achieve exceptional performance, it is occasionally necessary to step on the accelerator. In other words, those trades you really believe in, you play more aggressively. Of course, the tricky thing is doing this while still maintaining risk control. Obviously, you need both a high degree of confidence and accuracy to pull this off.

I discovered that a number of the extraordinarily successful traders failed a number of times and sometimes for an extended period before they finally put it all together.

If you were starting again, but know what you know now about trading, how would that change you?

This isn't like the question, "How would you live your life differently if you were 18 again?" That is a hypothetical question. In the case of trading, unless you are out of the game (i.e., broke), you can start again. In fact, in a way, you start again every day.

Has your trading changed as a result of your insights from The Market Wizards? If not, what do you think you need to do to produce the spectacular results that you'd like? What would you need to give up to become a top trader yourself? Are you willing to do it?

As I have only recently finished the book, it is far too early to say. Ironically, the period since I began working on the book has been my worst trading phase in recent years. Although there were, no doubt, other factors involved to some extent, I believe the strain of simultaneously working at a full-time job and doing this book had a detrimental impact on my trading. This may be a rationalization, but I think it's true.

How has my trading changed? Well, for one thing, the reinforcement of the discipline message has gotten me to become more methodical. I have just resumed keeping a trading diary, an exercise I knew from past experience was very valuable, but one that I had let lapse for many years. I have also started routinely reviewing multi-year charts every week, instead of haphazardly as I did before.

Another change is that I am now more conscious of the need to wait for the right trading opportunity and not feel you have to make a trade every day. Oddly enough, even though I consider myself a long-term trader, the desire to trade frequently has been a problem. Thinking of your own works and writings, I guess this might be a good example of what you call "conflict."

For example, I find that for myself, unplanned trades made at the spur of the moment during market hours are almost invariably losers. I am trying to keep myself from doing those trades. It is not as easy as it sounds because the lower risk (i.e., relatively close stop points) often associated with such trades makes them very alluring. The problem is their success rate is dismal. I believe that the reinforcement of the message of patience that I received in doing the book will eventually help me eliminate this personal flaw.

As to what I need to do to become a super trader, I don't think I know the answer. In fact, I am not even sure there is necessarily an answer. On a basic level, I don't agree with the premise of the question. It implies that any individual can achieve spectacular performance if he or she does the right things and avoids basic mistakes. This may be true to achieve profitable trading, but there is a vast difference between profitable trading and super trading. Excellence in trading, like excellence in any other field, is a blend of hard work (which is achievable) and talent (which you either have or don't have). I don't believe that most traders have the capability to become super traders.

Marathon running I believe provides a very appropriate analogy. Virtually anyone can run a marathon if they are willing to work hard enough at it. Even handicapped people can and have achieved this feat, which is an impossibility for the healthy but untrained individual. However, no matter how hard you train there will be some natural limit that you will not be able to exceed. Probably only a small percentage of the population has the physical makeup that would make a 2:10 marathon even a possibility. Of course, such a select individual would still have to do a remarkable amount of hard work to achieve that time. However, the rest of us can never achieve a 2:10 marathon no matter how hard we train. The limit of what is achievable will vary from individual to individual.

But for the sake of answering your question, assuming I had the capability, what would I need to give up to become a super trader? Judging by the history of most of the traders I interviewed, I would probably need to give up my job and devote myself full time to trading and trading-related analysis. Although I am very fortunate in that my job is related to trading — research director at a major brokerage firm — a great deal of my time is devoted to tasks that have nothing to do with trading, such as writing or editing all the reports turned out by my department, answering phone inquiries, and so on. If I were single, perhaps I might consider this alternative. But with a wife and three small children, I wouldn't even dream of taking this action, which I would consider gambling with their financial security and well being. Obviously, in my life, other things take priority over the goal of becoming a top trader. By the way, I don't mean to imply that by devoting myself full time to trading I would necessarily become a super trader. I am only answering your question as to what I think I would have to give up to achieve this goal and am unwilling to do.

*Van K. Tharp, Ph.D., 1410 E. Glenoaks Blvd., Glendale, CA 91206, (818) 241-8165, is a consultant to individual traders and trading companies. This interview is reprinted from his annual updates to the **Investment Psychology Guides**.*

References

Sweeney, John (1987), In search of the perfect system, *Technical Analysis of Stocks & Commodities, Volume 5: Trading Strategies,* p. 50.

Hartle, Thom (1989), Quick-Scan: Market Wizards: Interviews with Top Traders, *Technical Analysis of Stocks & Commodities,* September, p. 26.

Schwager, Jack (1984), *A Complete Guide to the Futures Market,* New York: John Wiley & Sons.

APPENDIX II

A Complete Record Of Trading Signals

The complete record since 1985 has been compiled for the Standard & Poor Stock Index Futures, U.S. Treasury Bonds, the German Mark and Crude Oil. First, markets eligible for trading have been identified in accordance with Chapters 6 to 9. Then trading formations and entry signals, as described in Chapters 4 and 5, have been applied. Liquidation of trades is assumed throughout in accordance with Chapter 13 (Stops and Liquidation of Trades).

S&P STOCK INDEX FUTURES: October 1985 to March 1991

Weekly Chart Trend Changes

Date	Trend	Months Duration	Trades
Oct. '85 - July '86	Up	8	7 Buys
August '86	Erratic	1	2 Buys
Sept. - Oct. '86	Down	2	1 Sell
Nov. - Dec. '86	Erratic	2	0
Jan. - May '87	Up	3	3 Buys
May - June '87	Erratic	2	0
June - Oct. '87	Up	3	2 Buys
Oct. - Nov. '87	Down	2	1 Sell
Nov. '87 - Nov. '88	Erratic	13	0
Nov. '88 - Oct. '89	Up	11	7 Buys
Oct. '89 - March '90	Down	5	1 Sell
April '90 - July '90	Up	3	4 Buys
July '90 - Jan. '91	Down	6	2 Sells
Jan. '91 - March '91	Up	3	1 Buy

Uptrend - 31 months
Downtrend - 15 months
Erratic - 18 months

S&P Trades

1. Oct. 11, 1985	Buy @ 187.20	
	Rule 2/W-Formation/Reverse Head and Shoulders	
Dec. 23	Sell @ 210.45	
	Stopped out	+23.25

2.	Dec. 27	Buy @ 212.20	
		Rule 3	
	Jan. 8, 1986	Sell @ 210.80	
		Stopped out	-1.40
3.	Feb. 7	Buy @ 216.80	
		Buy signal on the weekly chart/Rule 6	
	April 3	Sell @ 234.80	
		Stopped out	+18.00
4.	April 8	Buy @ 235.60	
		Rule 2	
	April 29	Sell @ 239.80	
		Stopped out	+4.20
5.	May 5	Buy @ 237.80	
		Rule 1	
	May 15	Sell @ 233.20	
		Stopped out	-4.60
6.	May 20	Buy @ 238.90	
		Rule 6	
	June 2	Sell @ 247.50	
		Stopped out	+8.60
7.	June 12	Buy @ 243.00	
		Rule 1	
	July 7	Sell @ 249.80	
		Stopped out	+ 6.80
8.	Aug. 12	Buy @ 244.20	
		Weekly upside reversal/Rule 2	
	Sept. 2	Sell @ 249.30	
		Stopped out	+5.10
9.	Sept. 3	Buy @ 250.80	
		Rule 6	
	Sept. 4	Sell @ 250.00	
		Major reversal against the trade at a double top	- .80
10.	Sept. 4	Sell @ 251.40	
		Triple top/M-Formation/Rule 5	
	Oct. 7	Buy @ 234.60	
		Second buy signal	+16.80
11.	Jan. 5, 1987	Buy @ 253.20	
		M-Formation/Rule 4	
	Jan. 23	Sell @ 275.80	
		Stopped out	+22.60
12.	Feb. 13	Buy @ 283.50	
		Rule 1	
	March 27	Sell @ 297.40	
		Major downside reversal	+13.90

13.	April 1	Buy @ 294.60 Rule 5	
	April 7	Sell @ 296.40 Major downside reversal	+1.80
14.	June 9	Buy @ 299.50 Break above the trendline/W-Formation/Rule 2	
	June 24	Sell @ 309.30 Gap filled on a closing basis	+9.80
15.	July 8	Buy @ 310.80 Rule 2	
	Aug. 28	Sell @ 327.50 Weekly downside reversal	+16.70
16.	Oct. 11	Sell @ 316.00 M-Formation/Weekly downside reversal/Rule 2	
	Oct. 20	Buy @ 222.50 Major closing price reversal	+93.50
17.	Jan. 11, 1989	Buy @ 287.60 Weekly upside reversal/Rule 5	
	Feb. 10	Sell @ 297.60 Weekly downside reversal	+10.00
18.	April 14	Buy @ 304.00 Rule 4	
	May 2	Sell @ 309.40 Weekly downside reversal/Rule 5	+5.40
19.	May 12	Buy @ 324.60 Weekly upside reversal/Rule 3	
	June 5	Sell @ 331.50 Gap filled on a closing basis	+6.90
20.	June 7	Buy @ 333.30 Rule 2	
	June 15	Sell @ 329.80 Stopped out	-3.50
21.	June 22	Buy @ 331.50 Rule 5	
	June 30	Sell @ 329.80 Stopped out	-1.70
22.	July 10	Buy @ 333.40 5 Up days/Rule 1	
	Aug. 16	Sell @ 351.40 Second sell signal	+18.00
23.	Aug. 22	Buy @ 347.50 Rule 6	
	Sept. 6	Sell @ 353.50 Stopped out	+6.00

24.	Oct. 1	Buy @ 355.00	
		Rule 5	
	Oct. 11	Sell @ 359.80	
		Stopped out	+4.80
25.	Jan. 9, 1990	Sell @ 352.00	
		Rule 5	
	Jan. 22	Buy @ 333.00	
		Major reversal	+19.00
26.	May 4	Buy @ 345.00	
		Rule 5	
	June 8	Sell @ 364.50	
		Weekly reversal	+19.50
27.	June 12	Buy @ 372.00	
		Rule 2	
	June 18	Sell @ 362.00	
		Major reversal	-10.00
28.	June 21	Buy @ 371.00	
		Rule 1	
	June 22	Sell @ 362.50	
		Major reversal	-8.50
29.	July 6	Buy @ 367.00	
		Rule 5	
	July 20	Sell @ 369.00	
		Weekly reversal	+2.00
30.	July 27	Sell @ 360.00	
		Rule 5 (Double Lindahl)	
	Aug. 27	Buy @ 327.00	
		Island Reversal	+33.00
31.	Sept. 13	Sell @ 322.00	
		Rule 5	
	Sept. 28	Buy @ 307.00	
		Major reversal	+15.00
32.	Jan. 27, 1991	Buy @ 339.50	
		Rule 3	
	March 14	Sell @ 374.00	
		Stopped out	+34.50

Trading Summary

(One contract per trade; no allowance for slippage or commissions)

Profitable Trades	25	78%	415.15 Points	$207,575
Losing Trades	7	22%	(30.50)	(15,250)
Total Trades	32	100%	384.65	$192,325

Average Profit $8,303   Average Loss $2,179   Average Trade $6,010

U.S. TREASURY BONDS: March 1985 to March 1991

Weekly Chart Trend Changes

Date	Trend	Months Duration	Trades
March '85 - July '85	Up	5	4 Buys
July '85 - Oct. '85	Down	4	1 Sell
Oct. '85 - Sept. '86	Up	11	4 Buys/1 Sell
Sept. '86 - Oct. '86	Erratic (Down)	2	1 Sell
Oct. '86 - March '87	Up	5	7 Buys/1 Sell
March '87 - June '87	Down	4	1 Sell
June '87 - Aug. '87	Erratic	3	1 Buy
Aug. '87 - Oct. '87	Down	2	1 Sell
Oct. '87 - Nov. '87	Up	2	1 Buy
Nov. '87	Down	1	1 Sell
Dec. '87 - March '88	Up	4	2 Buys
March '88 - Sept. '88	Down	5	2 Sells
Sept. '88 - March '89	Up	6	4 Buys
March '89 - May '89	Erratic	2	0
May '89 - Sept. '89	Up	5	3 Buys
Sept. '89	Down (Failed)	1	1 Sell
Oct. '89 - Dec. '89	Up	3	1 Buy
Dec. '89 - May '90	Down	6	5 Sells
May '90 - Oct. '90	Erratic	6	1 Buy/1 Sell
Oct. '90 - March '91	Up	6	4 Buys

Uptrend - 47 months
Downtrend - 23 months
Erratic - 13 months

U.S. Treasury Bond Trades

1. March 25, 1985   Buy @ 6726
   Double weekly reversal/W-Formation
     on the daily chart/Rule 5

   April 23   Sell @ 7012
   Gap filled at a potential top   +2.18

2.	May 10	Buy @ 7130	
		Rule 3	
	June 7	Sell @ 7620	
		Island reversal	+4.22
3.	June 14	Buy @ 7812	
		Rule 5	
	June 20	Sell @ 7702	
		Failure at double top/sell signal	-1.10
4.	July 5	Buy @ 7630	
		Rule 6	
	July 11	Sell @ 7502	
		Island reversal	-1.28
5.	July 11	Sell @ 7502	
		M-Formation/Rule 4	
	Aug. 1	Buy @ 7326	
		Gapped against the trade	+1.06
6.	Oct. 18	Buy @ 7224	
		Weekly reversal/5 days up/Break out of a triangle/Rule 1	
	Jan. 8, 1986	Sell @ 8208	
		Outside down day/limit down	+9.16
7.	Jan. 20	Buy @ 8220	
		Weekly reversal/Rule 1/Rule 3	
	March 5	Sell @ 9300	
		Island reversal	+10.20
8.	March 7	Buy @ 9320	
		Rule 6	
	April 1	Sell @ 10102	
		Major reversal	+7.14
9.	Aug. 7	Buy @ 9421	
		Turned at the trendline on the weekly chart/ Weekly reversal/Rule 8	
	Aug. 27	Sell @ 9816	
		Major reversal day/Gap closed	+3.27
10.	Sept. 2	Sell @ 9730	
		M-Formation/Limit Down/Rule 7	
	Sept. 24	Buy @ 9324	
		Stopped out	+4.06
11.	Oct. 14	Sell @ 9226	
		M-Formation/Rule 5	
	Oct. 21	Buy @ 9226	
		Gapped against the trade	0
12.	Oct. 21	Buy @ 9224	
		W-Formation/Rule 4	

	Nov. 6	Sell @ 9512 Gapped against the trade	+2.20
13.	Nov. 12	Buy @ 9504 Rule 1	
	Nov. 25	Sell @ 9716 Major reversal	+2.12
14.	Dec. 2	Buy @ 9828 Rule 3	
	Dec. 5	Sell @ 9726 Major reversal at potential double top	-1.02
15.	Dec. 8	Buy @ 9816 Rule 6	
	Dec. 11	Sell @ 9720 Major reversal	-.28
16.	Dec. 22	Buy @ 9902 Rule 5	
	Dec. 29	Sell @ 9800 Major reversal/Gap filled	-1.02
17.	Dec. 29	Sell @ 9800 M-Formation/Rule 4	
	Jan. 2, 1987	Buy @ 9828 Major reversal/Gap filled	-.28
18.	Jan. 2	Buy @ 9828 W-Formation/Rule 7	
	Jan. 14	Sell @ 9906 Outside down day at double top	+.10
19.	Feb. 18	Buy @ 9828 Rule 5	
	March 3	Sell @ 10012 Gap against the trade	+1.16
20.	March 27	Sell @ 9824 Triple top on the weekly and daily charts/ Weekly reversal/Rule 5	
	April 27	Buy @ 9008 Major reversal/Gap filled	+8.16
21.	Aug. 6	Buy @ 8916 W-Formation/Rule 5	
	Aug. 17	Sell @ 8908 Major reversal	-.08
22.	Aug. 27	Sell @ 8700 M-Formation/Rule 2	
	Oct. 20	Buy @ 8026 Limit up	+6.06

23.	Oct. 20	Buy @ 7914	
		Limit up/Climactic gap/Rule 7	
	Nov. 23	Sell @ 8700	
		Outside reversal day	+7.16
24.	Dec. 15	Buy @ 8426	
		W-Formation/Rule 3	
	Jan. 8, 1988	Sell @ 8510	
		Major reversal	+.16
25.	Jan. 15	Buy @ 8918	
		Rule 1	
	March 4	Sell @ 9216	
		Major reversal at double top	+2.30
26.	March 4	Sell @ 9216	
		M-Formation/Weekly reversal/Double top/ Rule 7	
	April 6	Buy @ 9006	
		Gap filled	+2.10
27.	April 11	Sell @ 8810	
		Rule 6	
	June 1	Buy @ 8524	
		Gapped against the trade	+2.18
28.	Sept. 30	Buy @ 8824	
		W-Formation/Weekly reversal/Rule 3	
	Nov. 4	Sell @ 8924	
		Weekly reversal	+1.00
29.	Dec. 6	Buy @ 8900	
		Rule 3	
	Dec. 14	Sell @ 8730	
		Major reversal	-1.02
30.	Dec. 20	Buy @ 8904	
		Rule 1	
	Jan. 3, 1989	Sell @ 8800	
		Gapped against the trade	-1.04
31.	Jan. 12	Buy @ 8910	
		Rule 5	
	Feb. 9	Sell @ 8916	
		Gapped against the trade	+.06
32.	May 12	Buy @ 9020	
		W-Formation/Rule 2	
	June 15	Sell @ 9510	
		Major outside reversal day	+4.22
33.	June 20	Buy @ 9516	
		Rule 6	

	July 17	Sell @ 9618 Weekly reversal/Sell signal	+1.02
34.	July 24	Buy @ 9714 Rule 1	
	Aug. 4	Sell @ 9724 Weekly reversal	+.10
35.	Sept. 20	Sell @ 9620 M-Formation/Rule 1	
	Oct. 4	Buy @ 9614 Second buy signal	+.06
36.	Oct. 4	Buy @ 9604 5 up days/Rule 1/Rule 3	
	Dec. 22	Sell @ 9918 Weekly reversal at multiple top	+3.14
37.	Dec. 22	Sell @ 9918 M-Formation/Weekly reversal at multiple top/ Broke trendline/Rule 1	
	Feb. 9, 1990	Buy @ 9424 Stopped out	+4.26
38.	Feb. 10	Sell @ 9330 Rule 6	
	Feb. 26	Buy @ 9324 Gap filled	+.06
39.	Feb. 28	Sell @ 9306 Rule 6	
	March 16	Buy @ 9226 Weekly reversal	+.12
40.	March 29	Sell @ 9220 Rule 6	
	April 4	Buy @ 9308 Major reversal	-.20
41.	April 16	Sell @ 9204 Rule 1	
	May 4	Buy @ 9024	+1.12
42.	Aug. 3	Sell @ 93.02 Rule 2	
	Aug. 30	Buy @ 89.04 Gap filled	+3.30
43.	Sept. 28	Buy @ 88.31 Rule 1	
	Oct. 9	Sell @ 88.23 Gap filled	-.08
44.	Oct. 16	Buy @ 89.09 Rule 1	

	Dec. 21	Sell @ 95.00	
		Stopped out	+5.23
45.	Dec. 31	Buy @ 95.09	
		Rule 5	
	Jan. 7, 1991	Sell @ 94.25	
		Gapped against the trade	-.16
46.	Jan. 17	Buy @ 96.03	
		Rule 6	
	Feb. 20	Sell @ 96.30	
		Stopped out	+.27
47.	March 14	Buy @ 95.20	
		Rule 5	
	March 19	Sell @ 93.14	
		Stopped out	-2.06

Trading Summary

(One contract per trade; no allowance for slippage or commissions)

Profitable Trades	33	70%	109.15 Points	$109,469
Losing Trades	14	30%	(13.02)	(13,062)
Total Trades	47	100%	96.13	$96,407

Average Profit $3,317   Average Loss $933   Average Trade $2,051

D-MARK: March 1985 to April 1991

Weekly Chart Trend Changes

Date	Trend	Months Duration	Trades
March '85 - July '87	Up	26	17 Buys/4 Sells
July '87 - Oct. '87	Erratic	3	0
Oct. '87 - Jan. '88	Up	3	3 Buys
Jan. 88 - April '88	Erratic	3	0
April '88 - Sept. '88	Down	6	2 Sells
Sept. '88 - Dec. '88	Up	4	2 Buys
Jan. '89 - Sept. '89	Down	9	3 Sells
Sept. '89 - Oct. '89	Erratic	2	1 Buy
Oct. '89 - Feb. '91	Up	16	13 Buys/1 Sell
Feb. '91 - April '91	Erratic	3	1 Sell

Uptrend - 50 months
Downtrend - 15 months
Erratic - 11 months

D-Mark Trades

1.	March 19, 1985	Buy @ 3185	
		Trendline crossed on the weekly chart/3-week island/Rule 3	
	April 29	Sell @ 3380	
		Gap filled	+195
2.	May 7	Buy @ 3220	
		Rule 4	
	May 28	Sell @ 3295	
		Gapped against the trade	+75
3.	June 17	Buy @ 3305	
		Rule 5	
	Aug. 30	Sell @ 3585	
		Major reversal	+280
4.	Sept. 20	Buy @ 3590	
		Rule 5	
	March 5, 1986	Sell @ 4485	
		Island reversal	+895
5.	April 8	Buy @ 4335	
		Rule 4	
	April 30	Sell @ 4600	
		Major reversal/outside down day	+265
6.	May 6	Buy @ 4585	
		Rule 6	
	May 16	Sell @ 4540	
		Gap against the trade	-45
7.	June 4	Buy @ 4440	
		Rule 4	
	June 17	Sell @ 4500	
		Gap against the trade	+60
8.	June 30	Buy @ 4530	
		Rule 6	
	July 11	Sell @ 4565	
		Weekly reversal at double top	+35
9.	July 21	Buy @ 4630	
		Rule 8	
	Sept. 2	Sell @ 4860	
		Gap against the trade	+230

10.	Sept. 6	Buy @ 4895	
		Rule 6	
	Sept. 23	Sell @ 4910	
		Gap against the trade	+15
11.	Sept. 29	Buy @ 4990	
		Rule 4	
	Oct. 23	Sell @ 5015	
		Gap against the trade	+25
12.	Nov. 7	Buy @ 4875	
		Rule 1	
	Dec. 5	Sell @ 5010	
		Major reversal/Gap filled	+135
13.	Dec. 12	Buy @ 4990	
		Weekly reversal/Rule 1	
	Jan. 20, 1987	Sell @ 5445	
		Island Reversal	+455
14.	Jan. 22	Buy @ 5555	
		Rule 4	
	Feb. 10	Sell @ 5550	
		Major reversal/Double top	-5
15.	Feb. 19	Buy @ 5515	
		Rule 6	
	March 16	Sell @ 5450	
		Major reversal and failure	-65
16.	March 16	Buy @ 5490	
		Rule 3	
	April 1	Sell @ 5505	
		Island reversal	+15
17.	April 1	Sell @ 5505	
		M-Formation/Rule 4	
	April 9	Buy @ 5530	+25
18.	April 9	Buy @ 5530	
		Rule 4	
	May 22	Sell @ 5625	
		Weekly reversal at double top	+95
19.	May 22	Sell @ 5680	
		Double weekly reversal at double top/ Rule 5	
	June 2	Buy @ 5615	
		Island reversal	+65
20.	June 12	Sell @ 5570	
		M-Formation/Rule 1	
	June 16	Buy @ 5500	
		Weekly reversal/Gap filled	+70

21.	July 17	Sell @ 5390 Rule 6	
	Aug. 18	Buy @ 5430 Gap against the trade	-40
22.	Oct. 8	Buy @ 5550 W-Formation/1-week island/Rule 4	
	Nov. 16	Sell @ 5855 Island reversal	+305
23.	Nov. 26	Buy @ 6040 Rule 1	
	Dec. 1	Sell @ 6115 Island reversal	+75
24.	Dec. 10	Buy @ 6190 Rule 1	
	Jan. 5, 1988	Sell @ 6170	-20
25.	April 21	Sell @ 6030 M-Formation/Rule 1	
	July 20	Buy @ 5420 Major reversal/Gap against the trade	+610
26.	July 26	Sell @ 5440 Rule 4	
	Aug. 11	Buy @ 5330 Weekly reversal/Second buy signal	+110
27.	Sept. 30	Buy @ 5390 W-Formation/Weekly reversal/Rule 5	
	Nov. 29	Sell @ 5830 Gap against the trade	+440
28.	Dec. 2	Buy @ 5880 Rule 6	
	Dec. 4	Sell @ 5810 Major reversal at double top	-70
29.	March 6, 1989	Sell @ 5445 M-Formation/Weekly reversal/Rule 1	
	April 4	Buy @ 5400 Gap against the trade	+45
30.	April 25	Sell @ 5430 Rule 1	
	May 24	Buy @ 5075 Gap against the trade	+355
31.	June 7	Sell @ 5105 Rule 5	
	June 15	Buy @ 5035 Major reversal/Gap filled	+70

32.	Sept. 18	Buy @ 5150	
		W-Formation/Weekly reversal/Rule 2	
	Oct. 6	Sell @ 5310	
		Major reversal/Outside down day	-160
33.	Oct. 12	Buy @ 5315	
		Rule 1	
	Nov. 9	Sell @ 5400	
		Gap filled	+85
34.	Nov. 13	Buy @ 5455	
		Rule 3	
	Jan. 3, 1990	Sell @ 5800	
		Gap filled	+345
35.	Jan. 4	Buy @ 5970	
		Rule 6	
	Jan. 19	Sell @ 5840	
		Broken trendline/Reversal	-130
36.	Jan. 26	Buy @ 5930	
		Rule 5	
	Feb. 15	Sell @ 5900	
		Gap against the trade	-30
37.	Feb. 16	Buy @ 5960	
		Rule 6	
	Feb. 25	Sell @ 5900	
		Gapped against the trade	-60
38.	March 3	Buy @ 5900	
		Rule 2	
	March 21	Sell @ 5860	
		Major reversal	-40
39.	March 29	Buy @ 5905	
		Rule 3	
	April 28	Sell @ 5880	
		Gapped against the trade	-25
40.	May 1	Buy @ 5965	
		Rule 5	
	May 17	Sell @ 6050	
		Gap filled	+85
41.	June 15	Buy @ 5925	
		Rule 8	
	Sept. 10	Sell @ 6310	
		Gapped against the trade	+385
42.	Sept. 13	Buy @ 6370	
	Dec. 3	Sell @ 6600	
		Stopped out	+230

43.	Dec. 7	Buy @ 6780	
		Rule 1	
	Dec. 18	Sell @ 6595	
		Gapped against the trade	-185
44.	Dec. 28	Buy @ 6675	
		Rule 1	
	Jan. 4, 1991	Sell @ 6615	
		Major reversal	-60
45.	Jan. 7	Sell @ 6490	
		Rule 3	
	Jan. 17	Buy @ 6620	
		Gapped against the trade	-130
46.	Jan. 18	Buy @ 6670	
		Rule 3	
	Feb. 19	Sell @ 6680	-10
		Gapped against the trade	
47.	Feb. 19	Sell @ 6640	
		Rule 1/Rule 4	
	April 1	Buy @ 5980	
		Gapped against the trade	+660

Trading Summary

(One contract per trade; no allowance for slippage or commissions)

Profitable Trades	31	66%	6,735 Points	$84,187
Losing Trades	16	34%	(1,075)	(13,437)
Total Trades	47	100%	5,660	$70,750

Average Profit $2,715   Average Loss $840   Average Trade $1,505

CRUDE OIL: July 1985 to March 1991

Weekly Chart Trend Changes

Date	Trend	Months Duration	Trades
July '85 - Nov. '85	Up	4	3 Buys/1 Sell
Nov. '85 - March '86	Down	4	1 Sell
March '86 - Dec. '86	Erratic	10	0
Dec. '86 - Aug. '87	Up	8	4 Buys
Aug. '87 - March '88	Down	7	4 Sells

March '88 - May '88	Up	2	3 Buys
June '88 - Oct. '88	Down	5	6 Sells
Nov. '88 - Jan. '90	Up	14	11 Buys
Jan. '90 - July '90	Down	7	6 Sells
Aug. '90 - Dec. '90	Up	5	4 Buys
Dec. '90 - March '91	Down	5	4 Sells

Uptrend - 33 months
Downtrend - 28 months
Erratic - 10 months

Crude Oil Trades

1.	July 24, 1985	Buy @ 2585	
		Rule 5 weekly buy signal/W-Formation on the daily chart/Rule 1	
	Sept. 5	Sell @ 2700	
		Island reversal	+115
2.	Sept. 5	Sell @ 2700	
		Weekly reversal at resistance/Rule 4	
	Sept. 12	Buy @ 2700	
		Closed gap	0
3.	Sept. 17	Buy @ 2695	
		Rule 5	
	Oct. 9	Sell @ 2830	
		Second sell signal/Exit Rule 4	+135
4.	Oct. 15	Buy @ 2760	
		Rule 1/Rule 3	
	Nov. 27	Sell @ 2890	
		Weekly reversal/Major daily reversal/ Limit down	+130
5.	Nov. 27	Sell @ 2890	
		Weekly reversal at historic high/Limit down/ Rule 7	
	Dec. 16	Buy @ 2600	
		(Rollover)	+290
6.	Dec. 16	Sell @ 2350	
		(Rollover)	
	March 21, 1986	Buy @ 1450	
		Triple reversal days	+900
7.	Dec. 11	Buy @ 1590	
		Rule 3	

	Feb. 11, 1987	Sell @ 1765	
		Gapped against the trade	+195
8.	March 3	Buy @ 1715	
		Rule 3	
	April 10	Sell @ 1750	
		Weekly reversal	+35
9.	April 15	Buy @ 1795	
		W-Formation/Rule 1	
	June 21	Sell @ 1950	
		Gapped against the trade	+155
10.	June 25	Buy @ 1765	
		Turn at the trendline/Rule 6	
	July 23	Sell @ 2120	
		Gap filled	+355
11.	Aug. 5	Sell @ 2130	
		M-Formation/Rule 4	
	Aug. 26	Buy @ 1945	
		Gap filled	+185
12.	Nov. 30	Sell @ 1850	
		Rule 1	
	Dec. 22	Buy @ 1615	
		Gap against the trade/Limit up	+235
13.	Jan. 11, 1988	Sell @ 1650	
		Rule 1	
	Jan. 14	Buy @ 1695	
		Major reversal	-45
14.	Feb. 10	Sell @ 1715	
		Rule 4	
	March 10	Buy @ 1600	
		Gap against the trade	+115
15.	March 18	Buy @ 1595	
		W-Formation/Weekly buy signal/Rule 3	
	April 4	Sell @ 1650	
		Gap against the trade	+55
16.	April 6	Buy @ 1675	
		Rule 2	
	April 19	Sell @ 1790	
		Island reversal	+155
17.	May 6	Buy @ 1770	
		Rule 1	
	June 8	Sell @ 1740	
		Gap against the trade	-30
18.	June 8	Sell @ 1740	
		M-Formation/Rule 3	

	June 14	Buy @ 1700	
		Gap against the trade	+40
19.	June 15	Sell @ 1715	
		Rule 6	
	July 18	Buy @ 1590	
		Gap against the trade	+125
20.	July 26	Sell @ 1620	
		Rule 6	
	July 28	Buy @ 1645	
		Major reversal	-25
21.	Aug. 2	Sell @ 1595	
		Rule 2	
	Aug. 5	Buy @ 1575	
		Island reversal	+20
22.	Aug. 25	Sell @ 1540	
		Rule 3	
	Sept. 12	Buy @ 1430	
		Major reversal	+110
23.	Sept. 15	Sell @ 1460	
		Rule 4	
	Oct. 12	Buy @ 1375	
		Island reversal	+85
24.	Nov. 22	Buy @ 1370	
		W-Formation/Rule 4	
	Jan. 23, 1989	Sell @ 1730	
		Major reversal	+400
25.	Feb. 1	Buy @ 1665	
		Rule 6	
	Feb. 6	Sell @ 1610	
		Major reversal	-55
26.	Feb. 7	Buy @ 1635	
		Rule 6/ Rule 8	
	Feb. 10	Sell @ 1595	
		Stopped out	-40
27.	Feb. 15	Buy @ 1645	
		Rule 5	
	March 31	Sell @ 1900	
		Major reversal/Gaps filled	+255
28.	April 10	Buy @ 1825	
		Rule 1	
	April 13	Sell @ 1780	
		Major reversal	-45
29.	April 14	Buy @ 1825	
		Rule 6	

	April 24	Sell @ 1825	
		Major reversal	0
30.	Aug. 10	Buy @ 1810	
		Rule 3	
	Sept. 22	Sell @ 1910	
		Major reversal	+100
31.	Sept. 25	Buy @ 1930	
		Rule 6	
	Oct. 23	Sell @ 1975	
		Major reversal	+45
32.	Dec. 1	Buy @ 1990	
		Weekly reversal/Breakout/Rule 1	
	Jan. 4, 1990	Sell @ 2200	
		Major reversal	+210
33.	Jan. 10	Buy @ 2200	
		Rule 2	
	Jan. 15	Sell @ 2150	
		Major reversal	-50
34.	Jan. 25	Buy @ 2025	
		Rule 1	
	Feb. 5	Sell @ 2080	
		Gapped against the trade	+55
35.	April 5	Sell @ 2005	
		Rule 1	
	April 19	Buy @ 1910	
		Major Reversal	+95
36.	April 17	Sell @ 1905	
		Rule 6	
	April 19	Buy @ 1940	
		Gap filled	-35
37.	April 25	Sell @ 1920	
		Rule 3	
	May 1	Buy @ 1950	
		Gap filled	-30
38.	May 10	Sell @ 1860	
		Rule 8	
	May 16	Buy @ 1995	
		Weekly reversal	-135
39.	May 18	Sell @ 1940	
		Rule 5	
	June 12	Buy @ 1750	
		Gapped against the trade	+190
40.	June 15	Sell @ 1885	
		Rule 2	

	July 12	Buy @ 1860	
		Gapped against the trade	+25
41.	July 17	Buy @ 2060	
		Rule 5	
	Aug. 27	Sell @ 2580	
		Gapped against the trade	+520
42.	Sept. 4	Buy @ 2855	
		Rule 4	
	Oct. 2	Sell @ 3400	
		Gapped against the trade	+545
43.	Oct. 3	Buy @ 3255	
		Rule 6	
	Oct. 17	Sell @ 3190	
		Double reversal against the trade	-65
44.	Oct. 24	Buy @ 3015	
		Rule 4	
	Nov. 5	Sell @ 2920	
		Gapped against the trade	-95
45.	Dec. 2	Sell @ 2590	
		Rule 2	
	Dec. 27	Buy @ 2425	
		Gap filled	+165
46.	Jan. 2, 1991	Sell @ 2350	
		Rule 6	
	Jan. 7	Buy @ 2405	
		Gapped against the trade	-55
47.	Jan. 15	Sell @ 2500	
		Rule 6	
	March 4	Buy @ 1955	
		Gapped against the trade	+545
48.	March 7	Sell @ 1885	
		Rule 2	
	March 12	Buy @ 1905	
		Major reversal	-20

Trading Summary

(One contract per trade; no allowance for slippage or commissions)

Profitable Trades	32	67%	6,545 Points	$65,450
Losing Trades	16	33%	(725)	(7,250)
Total Trades	48	100%	5,820	$58,200

Average Profit $2,450   Average Loss $453   Average Trade $1,215